Praise for:

I am Not Sick I Don't Need Help!

Helping the Seriously Mentally Ill Accept Treatment.

At last we have a volume for those individuals most closely associated with the mentally ill. In a very readable fashion, Dr. Amador addresses the nature of patients' unawareness of their illness and their need for treatment. He also clearly outlines the relevant research and gives clear prescriptions to help families and therapists deal with patients' obliviousness to their condition. I strongly recommend this to families and therapists of individuals with serious mental illness.

AARON T. BECK, M.D. *Emeritus Professor of Psychiatry, University of Pennsylvania, Department of Psychiatry*

This is the first book to address the elephantine question running roughshod over families of individuals with schizophrenia and bipolar disorder: *Why won't the sick person take his/her medicine?* Amador, a psychologist who has a brother with schizophrenia, has pioneered research on poor insight into illness, a.k.a. anosognosia, for the past decade and is an acknowledged authority on it. He blends clinical vignettes skillfully with his erudition, and the resulting mix is both edible and edifying. Most important, Amador provides families and mental health professionals with a concrete, step-by-step plan to improve awareness of illness. This book fills a tremendous void in the literature on schizophrenia and bipolar disorder.

E. FULLER TORREY, M.D.
Author of Surviving "Schizophrenia."

Looking back, the strangest part was not the omnipresent government agents, the agonizing radiation weapons, or even my own super hero-like capabilities. What frightens me most is that my manic depression gave me an immovable certainty that it was the world around me that was convulsing but that my perception and judgment of it were unaltered. Thinking of this time leaves me frustrated and embarrassed as well as apprehensive that it might come again.

I read Dr. Amador's book and felt better. First, he concretely and understandably establishes that most denials of treatment are but manifestations of the illness and that it is the illness that is the enemy. Dr. Amador then presents a powerful game plan for penetrating, or at least circumventing, sickness induced lack of insight that will maximize the cooperation with treatment of those affected. When I first became ill, I wish this book had been in the hands of someone who cared about me.

JONATHAN STANLEY, JD *Assistant Director, Treatment Advocacy Center and, a Consumer diagnosed with Bipolar Disorder*

There are several publications that address best practices for clinicians treating persons with schizophrenia. These are written from the perspective of the practitioner. There are a few books written from the perspective of the consumer or of the family member, but these do not incorporate the values of clinical insights, particularly those reflecting recent research findings. The great value of "I am Not Sick, I Don't Need Help" is that it incorporates both the consumer's perspective and that of the clinician. It finds common ground, pointing out where the consumer and his/her clinician can work together in partnership. It is practical, easy to read, and hopeful. I highly recommend it to anyone interested in helping those who, like myself, live with the condition we call schizophrenia.

FREDERIC J. FRESE III, Ph.D. *Summit County Recovery Project and, a Consumer diagnosed with Schizophrenia*

Of the myriad of problems presented by serious mental illness Dr. Amador has focused on the single most critical factor. Breakthroughs in treatment will not be effective unless we deal with medication noncompliance and the related issue of poor insight into illness. Dr. Amador takes this issue on in "I am Not Sick I Don't Need Help" and deals with it head-on, providing vital information and practical advice for both families and therapists of patients with schizophrenia and bipolar disorder. This book will be immensely helpful to anyone dealing with the problems of medication noncompliance and poor insight.

MICHAEL FLAUM, M.D. *Director of Mental Health, State of Iowa*

This is a wonderful book bringing together the personal experiences of a psychologist and a lay person who have relatives with serious mental illness. Dr. Amador's research and clinical experience makes this book a rich source of information and practical advice. It is one of the salutary characteristics of our culture that people who experience pain convert that pain into something productive. People who are victimized by, stressed by, and dismayed by serious mental illness will find this book enormously helpful. It contains information about new research and concrete advice that will be of enormous help to both the families of the seriously mentally ill and to the mental health professionals who care for them.

HERBERT PARDES, M.D.
President, New York-Presbyterian, The University Hospital of Columbia and Cornell and, past Director of the National Institute of Mental Health

"I am Not Sick, I Don't Need Help!" is essential reading material for family members battling with their mentally ill loved ones about the need for treatment. Dr. Amador provides an insightful, compassionate, and practical guide for handling the frustration and guilt that inevitably arises when dealing with a sick individual who, by virtue of their illness, is completely unaware of the need for treatment.

What makes this book especially poignant is Dr. Amador's inclusion of his own personal account of his lifelong struggle with his own brother who suffers from schizophrenia, as well as his detailed presentations of patient cases. He does an exceptional job summarizing the compelling science behind poor insight, or anosognosia, clarifying that the loved one's lack of insight is not a product of a psychological defense mechanism, but is a result of the very brain dysfunction that underlies the illness. Practical tips on how to help a loved one with poor insight accept treatment or how to proceed with civil commitment, if necessary, make this book especially useful.

MICHAEL B. FIRST, M.D.
Editor, Diagnostic and Statistical Manual for Mental Disorders, Fourth Edition (DSM-IV)

This is a well-written and must-read practical guide for those facing serious mental illness in a loved one, friend, or colleague. Delusions and psychotic thinking are quite beyond our everyday experiences, so it is not surprising that most people are at a loss about how to approach and obtain help for someone with serious mental illness. Those with psychosis may not even recognize that their own behavior and function is disturbed, let alone that they need treatment. If only the ailment were a stomachache rather than a malady in the part of the brain that distinguishes normal from abnormal!

DOLORES MALASPINA, M.D. *Professor of Psychiatry, Columbia University College of Physicians and Surgeons, and Director, Clinical Neurobiology in Medical Genetics.*

For so many, it is very difficult to accept the notion that people like Ted Kaczynski or Anna-Lisa Johanson's mother have medical illnesses. It is easier to somehow cordon them off in our minds, just like they have been walled off from society through the centuries, as somehow less human than the rest of us. In this book, Dr. Amador breaks through these walls with personal courage and brilliant science.

Lack of insight in people with schizophrenia and bipolar disorder is the major cause of many of the worst aspects of their illness, and may be the most recalcitrant since it is difficult to treat someone who thinks that nothing is wrong. Dr. Amador has spent the better part of two decades conducting research on this topic and has been the world's most influential scientist in this important area of work. In this book, he prescribes detailed interventions to help families and therapists deal with lack of insight and the many difficulties it causes people with major mental illness. Yet Amador is not an academic preaching from an ivory tower. His poignant personal experiences with people with schizophrenia, including his brother and close friend, are laced throughout this thoughtful, moving, and indispensable book. "I am Not Sick, I Don't Need Help!" is an essential guide to anyone who knows, loves or treats someone with schizophrenia or bipolar disorder.

RICHARD KEEFE, PH.D. *Professor of Psychology in Psychiatry, Duke University Medical Center and, author of "Understanding Schizophrenia."*

It is uncommon to find books that bring together the latest findings in psychiatry research with relevant and practical clinical advice. Even less common are those that do so in a readable and engaging fashion, for both families and mental health professionals. Dr. Amador accomplishes all of the above in "I am Not Sick I Don't Need Help!"

ROBERTO GIL, M.D. *Director, Schizophrenia Research Unit at Columbia University and the New York State Psychiatric Institute.*

I Am Not Sick, I Don't Need Help!

Helping the seriously mentally ill accept treatment

A Practical Guide for:
Families and Therapists

by

Xavier Amador, Ph.D.
with Anna-Lisa Johanson

Books for Life®
VIDAPRESS

FIRST EDITION

Amador, Xavier, 1959 -
I AM NOT SICK I DON'T NEED HELP! Helping the Seriously Mentally Ill Accept Treatment. A Practical Guide for Families and Therapists / Xavier Amador. - 1st ed.
ISBN: 0-9677189-0-2

© Vida Press, L.L.C.

Vida Press
1150 Smith Road
Peconic, New York, 11958
www.VidaPress.com

To

Enrique and Margaret Mary

Contents

Proceeds (10% of the sale price) are donated to the:

National Alliance for the Mentally Ill,

National Alliance for Research on Schizophrenia and Depression,

National Depressive and Manic-Depressive Association,

and the

Albany Branch of the Community Foundation.

Foreword

Laurie Flynn
Executive Director, National Alliance for the Mentally Ill

"I'm Not Sick; I Don't Need Help!" addresses one of the toughest and most emotional problems in delivering mental health services. Dr. Xavier Amador and Anna-Lisa Johanson tackle this challenge by drawing on their own painful personal experience. The book offers a sensitive presentation of a practical, clinically sound, approach to getting a severely ill person to accept needed treatment.

Written in a respectful tone, the book provides clear, concrete guidance to families and professionals. Skillful use of case examples enlivens the text, which is filled with difficult "real world" situations. The focus throughout is on building mutual understanding and trust, so involuntary treatment can be avoided, if possible.

I hope this book will be widely read. It gives us a much-needed and long overdue common ground for helping people in crisis.

Foreword

Connie Lieber
President, National Alliance for Research on
Schizophrenia and Depression

There is probably no more difficult or more important responsibility for a family member in our society than meeting the needs of a mentally ill child, sibling or close relative. Daily life can be a struggle and the future impenetrable with uncertainty. Dr. Amador has taken up the challenge of guiding the family member in order to bring a better life to the afflicted patient and the responsible relatives. The unique combination of sensitivities he brings to this task reflect both his life experience as a sibling of an afflicted brother and his many years of broad clinical practice.

Reflecting his own profound empathy and insight, the book is a guide to the shocked, bewildered and too often hopeless close relative. It is no mere compendium of generalizations. It is a practical, step-by-step, program for achieving understanding and even expressing love in a situation where that love is difficult to convey.

His is a remarkable achievement and a great public service. Many lives of patients and their loved ones could be enhanced, often immeasurably if copies of this book were given to the families of every patient who begins to show signs of psychosis. As people use this book, it will mark the beginning of a sound remediation and even rehabilitation.

Foreword

Frederic J. Frese III, Ph.D.
Clinical Assistant Professor of Psychology in Psychiatry,
Northeast Ohio Universities College of Medicine; and a
Consumer diagnosed with Schizophrenia

In March of 1966, I was a young Marine Corps security officer. I was responsible for guarding atomic weapons at a large Naval Air base and had just been selected for promotion to the rank of Captain. One day, during a particularly stressful period, I made a "discovery" that certain high-ranking American officials had been hypnotized by our Communist enemies and were attempting to compromise this country's nuclear capabilities.

Shortly after deciding to reveal my discovery, I found myself locked away in the seclusion room of the base's psychiatric ward, diagnosed with schizophrenia. This was the beginning of my official life as a person with serious mental illness.

After about six months I was released from the psychiatric ward at the U.S. Naval Hospital at Bethesda, Maryland, and from the Marine Corps. During the following ten years I was repeatedly re-hospitalized and released from a variety of psychiatric facilities around the country. Most of these hospitalizations were involuntary.

Despite these adventures with schizophrenia breakdowns, I was somehow able to earn a doctorate in psychology. Subsequently, I have spent some twenty years working in Ohio's largest state hospital, caring for persons with disabilities similar to my own. For a long time, I told no one, except my immediate superiors, about my condition.

During all the time that I worked *incognito*, I was continuously struck by how little credibility patients had with my fellow staff members. Patients' points-of-view were almost always summarily discounted. They were to be cared for, but in a manner the staff saw as appropriate. In short, patients' opinions mattered little if their views differed from those of their caretakers.

About fifteen years ago some of us from around the country who had been in treatment for schizophrenia and other forms of serious mental illness began coming out of the shadows and identifying ourselves. We were no longer willing to remain hiding, quietly suffering the ridicule and hostility that too often characterize peoples' reactions to serious mental illness. Slowly, we began to organize, forming local, state, and then national organizations for recovering persons and our allies. We advocated, trying to regain our rights as human beings. For the most part, the more articulate consumer-advocates felt that professionals, who so readily dismissed our point-of-view when we had been patients, were not to be trusted. Many of us felt we could make it on our own. And why not? All of us had been diagnosed with having serious mental illnesses, but most of us were quite sure there was nothing wrong with us. During the early years, after being diagnosed, I was quite certain there was nothing wrong with me.

About twelve years ago, however, some consumer-advocates began to suggest that many of us, particularly those who were most disabled, could not so easily make it "on our own." We suggested that most of us did indeed need other people: family members, friends, and often the help of experienced mental health professionals. However, when we do find ourselves in need of these professionals, we are lucky if we find ourselves with any who are willing to work as *partners*, treating us as equals in trusting, mutually respectful relationships.

Although the ideal partnership may sound like a worthy goal, in practice, it can be exceedingly difficult for a professional to "partner" with a person whose condition dictates that nothing is wrong with him. I must admit that I have always felt somewhat inadequate in making recommendations in this regard. I usually warn questioners that it is not wise to try and argue with the patient regarding what appear to be delusional or illogical beliefs. But I have never been able to spell out a specific plan as to how to find common ground with a person whose condition renders him incapable of understanding that he has an illness.

This is one of the reasons I am particularly impressed by "I am Not Sick, I Don't Need Help!" In this book, Dr. Amador lays out a specific plan of attack that addresses this difficult problem. It is an effective strategy for finding common ground that can be used to build trust and cooperation for mutually addressing the problems of the patient. The justification and description of the "listen-empathize-agree-partnership" approach rings true to this person who "has been there." Particularly valuable is the recommendation that clinicians and relatives not openly challenge the beliefs of the mentally ill person. Unfortunately such challenging is still quite common and is frequently justified by the thought that "you should not buy into the belief system" of a delusional person.

Such thinking among mental health providers is misguided. What is important, particularly during the initial stages of interaction is that professionals afford dignity to those in their care. How important it is to communicate respect.

Throughout this volume I was pleased to see that Dr. Amador's recommendations reflected both common sense and up-to-date knowledge of serious brain-based mental illnesses as opposed to a blind adherence to traditional clinical dogma. For instance, he strongly recommends that efforts be made to involve family members in treatment. Undoubtedly, Dr. Amador's own experience with his brother who has schizophrenia, has taught him the value of this approach. Dr. Amador also recommends working closely with the police when involuntary treatment becomes necessary, particularly if they function in a manner similar to that of the Memphis Tennessee crisis intervention team. Again, this is very good advice.

Of particular importance is the section on commitment. Unfortunately there are times when it is best for all concerned for a floridly psychotic person to be given treatment against his stated wishes. Indeed, I might not be alive today if I had not been picked up by the police and taken to a hospital, although I certainly resisted at the time. And during my three decades as a treating psychologist I have certainly known numerous patients who were later to be most thankful that they had received effective treatment despite their adamant protests at the time it was being forecbly delivered.

Toward the end of the book, the reader is offered a plethora of useful information. A list of supportive organizations, with contact information, is given in Chapter 14. This is followed by a list of literature cited and reccomended readings. The appendix contains an excellent synopsis of inpatient and outpatient commitment laws for every state and the District of Columbia. This is followed by an annotated bibilography of recently published research studies which focus on the role of insight in mental illness.

In addition to describing effective strategies for dealing with mentally ill persons and providing a list of helpful resources, Dr. Amador provides delightful anecdotes that emphasize his main points and illustrate his suggestions. These serve as excellent mechanisms for tying his recommendations to the realities of trying to help mentally ill persons. Finally, Dr. Amador's and Ms. Johanson's willingness to share their personal experiences with their mentally ill loved ones make this book especially readable and poignant.

I hope you will be as impressed as I am with this book's approach to treatment for persons with serious mental illness. I strongly applaud Dr. Amador for working out these treatment strategies and for the sage advice he gives for persons involved in what continues to be one of the most challenging and perplexing arenas in modern health care.

Preface

Xavier Amador

Having never stepped foot inside a psychiatric ward, I felt nervous and self-conscious. Nervous for the same reasons most people are made uneasy when surrounded by twenty or so people with serious mental illness. Some of them were pacing and talking aloud to the voices they alone heard. Others were passionately smoking cigarettes. One man sat quietly, directly in front of me, his eyes fixed on some far away vision. Was I safe? Were they safe? Was this a hell hole or a haven ? These were just a few of the anxious thoughts running through my mind during the first of what would ultimately be countless days and nights in wards such as this one. I was feeling self conscious because I was sure I was somehow going to be blamed for what happened to my brother. Not the illness. But for the police, ambulance and restraints he endured because of me. No, I was confident my brother wouldn't blame me for the illness because as far as he was concerned there was nothing wrong with him. As he put it "I am not the one with the problem, you are!"

Many experiences converged to make me a clinical psychologist and schizophrenia researcher. But it goes without saying that my love for my brother Henry, or "Enrique" as he was known long before he became ill, was by far the most important.

Over the past ten years my colleagues and I have conducted research on the problem of poor insight into illness and treatment refusal in people with serious mental illness. After publishing the results of this work in scientific journals, I was frequently invited to give talks to family groups and a wide range of professional audiences all over the world. Among the things that the family members and health professionals had in common with me were feelings of frustration and helplessness that come when trying to help someone who fervently believes they don't need help. But one reaction that I was always surprised by, despite the fact that it happened nearly every time I spoke about the new research, was the excitement and hope sparked by the information

I had to share.

Hopefully this blatant lack of empathy with my audience can be forgiven as I have been studying the problem for well over ten years, reading all I could get my hands on, and conducting research of my own. It was so familiar to me that it no longer felt like the breakthrough that families and therapists in the audience were experiencing. But something changed recently. Perhaps it was the rash of killings by people with schizophrenia that hit the headlines, or a talk I gave at the annual conference of the National Alliance for the Mentally Ill. After my lecture I was surrounded at the podium and spoke for nearly two hours with family members who wanted advice and a greater understanding of why their loved one refused to accept help. The yearning of these people to learn more and to talk to someone who understood their frustration was enlightening to me. I was also struck by the realization that certain scientific advances, I was familiar with, hadn't yet reached many of the people who would benefit most from what has been learned. That is why I wrote this book.

This book was written for the families of the seriously mentally ill and for the mental health professionals who must work together to preserve the health, safety and future of people suffering from these brain disorders. Whether you are a family member or a therapist, in this book you will find hope in what the new research is revealing about the problem of poor insight into illness in schizophrenia and manic-depression. You probably have a theory about why the person you are concerned about "denies" being ill and refuses to take medication. But if you keep an open mind, you may be surprised by what science has uncovered about the causes of this problem. Knowledge is power and the more you know about denial of illness, the better equipped you'll be to deal with it and the refusal to accept treatment that it leads to. Prepare to be surprised and to have new hope. There is much you can do to conquer denial.

There are several people I want to thank for their help with this book. First, the parents of a young man with schizophrenia who first asked me to write it nearly five years ago. They wanted to learn more about the problem and how they could best deal with it. At that time the only literature I could offer them was in scientific journals and not one article was written to provide practical advice. The psychiatric residents, psychology interns, and social work students that I have supervised also deserve my gratitude. Without their enthusiasm for understanding the people whose care they were intrusted with, I would never have had to translate research findings into practical advice they could use in their clinical work.

I especially want to thank the countless people with serious mental illness who have opened up to me over the past two decades and taught me about their experience of having a serious mental illness. Many of them have enlightened me on what it is like to believe that one is not mentally ill, nor in need of treatment, when just about everybody else thinks otherwise.

Many organizations have supported the research described in this book. I want to thank them for their support and for their commitment to research on serious mental illness. My thanks to the National Alliance for Research on Schizophrenia and Affective Disorders (NARSAD), the Stanley Research Foundation, the Scottish Rite Foundation, the National Institute of Mental Health (NIMH), the National Depression and Manic Depression Association (NDMDA), and the National Alliance for the Mentally Ill (NAMI). I want to express my thanks to Scott Yale who has been indispensable these past ten years. Without his expertise and hard work, much of the research would not yet be completed. Thanks to Jodie for her enthusiastic support and to "O.K. Katie" for being there for me throughout the entire process.

Thanks also to E. Fuller Torrey, Connie Lieber, Jean Endicott, Harold Sackeim, Jack Gorman, Tom McGlashan, and Nancy Andreasen for their encouragement and support of the research.

Stacie Amador's faith in me, and in the value of what I had to say, has been a constant source of encouragement. Her love for Henry and the pleasure she takes in his company, has strengthened my faith in the capacity of people to look beyond mental illness to see the person hidden beneath. Lew Korman's confidence in my ideas and ability helped whenever my confidence in this project wavered. Various people helped more directly with the completion of this book by contributing their ideas and labor: Mary Zdanowicz, Jonathon Stanley, Rosanna Esposito, and Tom Brondolo.

I also want to thank David Kaczynski for his friendship and for sharing with me his thirst for knowledge about serious mental illness. His soul searching questions about Ted, a man who had been a kind and supportive brother when they were children, inspired me to finally begin work on this book.

Very special thanks to Anna-Lisa Johanson for all her hard work, enthusiastic support, and friendship. This book would have taken substantially longer to complete if not for Anna-Lisa. She did the lion's share of the research for the chapters on assisted treatment and commented extensively on the entire book. She interviewed families and helped me write several chapters. Whenever I wavered, whenever I procrastinated, she was there to push me along (on my answering machine, my email in box, and pager service). She worried that she had become a pest. I have thought of her more as a coach who wouldn't let me get away with anything short of my personal best. Thank you Anna-Lisa. Throughout our work together this past year she has also helped me to keep my original focus: to provide a practical resource for people who are trying to help someone with serious mental illness accept treatment.

Anna-Lisa's mother, who was variably diagnosed with either schizophrenia or manic depression, took her own life a little over one year ago. This tragedy had at least one positive outcome. It released Anna from a prison of shame she had been living in. We met when we were both interviewed for a television program about the life of her mother. Like so many of us with serious mental illness in the family, she had been ashamed by her mother's mental disorder. More precisely, she was embarrassed by the things her mother did when she was psychotic and like so many family members, tried to hide her mother's illness from her friends and peers.

Margaret Mary Ray, Anna-Lisa's mother, became famous because of the things her delusions led her to do. Anna agreed to write a magazine article about her mother and to be interviewed for television. Her objective was to provide balance to what the nation was hearing about the woman who had given her life and so much love. We were interviewed on the same day, in the same studio, and I recall that after my interview she came up to me to ask me questions about the illness her mother had suffered from.

She was particularly interested in what I had to say about poor insight into illness and treatment refusal. I was as amazed by her lack of knowledge about the illness that took her mother's life as I was by her courage and desire to learn. Anna-Lisa has been a source of inspiration and a constant reminder of how a little knowledge can go a long way. Although it came too late to help Margaret Mary Ray get the treatment that was so badly needed, what Anna learned has helped make her feel proud of her mother rather than ashamed. Like me, she feels an obligation to share that knowledge with others who could benefit from it.

Xavier Amador
March, 2000

Preface

Anna-Lisa Johansson

The opportunity to work with Xavier on this book has changed my perspective on mental illness and on the role one can take in securing treatment for a loved one. I hope that it will help people who are in the position I was. Unfortunately, I am one of the many people filled with helpless regret because I wasn't able to save my mother who had a serious mental illness. My mother made national headlines because one of her delusions was that she was married to David Letterman. She attracted publicity and an infamy that alienated those who could have helped her. A little over one year ago, my mother ended her life by throwing herself in front of a train.

Before my mother committed suicide, she had been sick for over twenty-five years. She first became ill several years before I was born, and in all that time she never once signed herself into a hospital voluntarily. Even more surprising to me now, is the fact that no one in our family and none of her friends ever had her committed to a hospital. Of all the close friends and family members who loved her, no one had the emotional strength and wherewithal to have her committed. Many people try to console me by saying how sad it was that she was so sick, but they saw no way to help her. The people who loved my mother claimed that they respected her freedom and her control over her life. No one felt they had the right to have her committed.

Throughout my childhood, my mother and I lived with friends or relatives who wanted to help her. I remember times when the family member we were staying with would make her seeing a therapist a condition of their support. By that time she was so sick, and suffered from such a lack of insight into her illness, that she was not able to accept treatment. In retrospect I can think of half a dozen times when someone could have called the police for help and had my mother involuntarily hospitalized.

All she needed was a few weeks of medication to stabilize her condition and give her a chance at a better life, but no one wanted to impose their will on her. I also think that no one wanted to invite the chaos they imagined would follow from involving the police. I remember when she was very sick she could become uncontrollable in her rage. Although I was a child at the time, I could easily understand why the adults around me were so reluctant to face the possibility of having that rage focused on them. That reluctance and misguided respect for her wishes led my mother to spend years homeless and ultimately to take her own life. It was easier to hope that if she was left alone she would calm down and somehow magically get better.

The good intentions of not violating my mother's personal sovereignty only led to a worsening of her condition. I was too young to know that there was anything that could be done to help my mother. I ended up spending the later years of childhood with my father because my mother was eventually found to be unfit to have custody of children.

As the child of someone who suffered from schizophrenia for years before taking her own life, I will always struggle with the guilt and anger that none of us had the influence to convince my mother to get help or, tried to have her committed when she refused the help she so badly needed. Maybe if we understood serious mental illness better than we did, we could have made a difference.

In retrospect, I now see that there were many points in her life where someone could have intervened to give her the medication that would help her battle the illness. Given the nature of mental illnesses, the proclivity for people to run away from their families and even worse, to commit suicide, there is a balance between the fear of facing the betrayal that you anticipate from your loved one and the regret that can last a lifetime if you do not act on your instincts.

When my mother died, my name appeared in newspapers across the country. My family tried very hard to hide from the media and to distance themselves from what had happened. I made a few tentative steps to try and change the picture of my mother that was being played on the news. I wanted to say that even though she was sick, she was a wonderful mother and had not always been "David Letterman's stalker." At first, I was so afraid of how people would look at me if they knew my mother was "crazy."

Then I realized how many other people suffered from mental illness. One-by-one, acquaintances, friends, and people I didn't even know, started to write to me or tell me about their experiences with a mentally ill family member. I realized then that my tragedy was one that is repeated every day. I am no longer embarrassed by my mother, instead, I'm very proud of her and embarrassed by the ignorance my family and I had about mental illness.

Everyone reading this book has a story to share that I know mirrors my own in many respects. The details may differ, but the themes are all very similar. The story of how untreated mental illness devastated our family is better known, but no more poignant than the millions of other families in this country who are dealing with a mentally ill loved one. I wanted to work on this book because I love my mother and wanted to share some lessons I learned, lessons that came with too high a price. Even though this book is too late to save her, it is not to late to help others. My mother was the kind of person who could see the silver lining in any cloud. I know that she would be proud of me for finding hope and purpose from the tragedy that struck our family. She was the kind of mother who would have been proud of my work on this book even though she never believed she was ill. I am her legacy.

I would like to thank Xavier for giving me the opportunity to be a part of this book and for showing me that mentally ill people need our advocacy, not our embarrassment and disdain. Both my work on this book and a new focus for my career were unexpected outgrowths of the tragedy of my mother's illness. This past year I made the decision to use my law degree to do advocacy work for the mentally ill, to change laws that unfairly ignore the needs of the millions of people who had the bad luck to develop a serious mental illness. I want to thank the Treatment Advocacy Center for supporting me in my career path and for showing me how much you can do with a law degree. I want to also thank my team of editors for being critical and my family for being understanding.

My husband Evan has my deepest gratitude. He has been a steady source of support and strength, both in my work on this book and in my mourning the loss of my mother. He has stood by my side as I've opened new doors and his love and encouragement has helped me to walk through them. I am grateful for the support and encouragement of all my families: the Johansons, the Cobbs, the Komps and the Rikhyes.

Finally, I want to thank my mother for all her love, she was beautiful and gave me life. When I think of her, I think of the person, not the illness she had. This book will help you to do the same and in the process, become more effective at battling the illness.

Anna-Lisa Johanson
March, 2000

Whilst part of what we perceive comes through our senses from the object before us, another part (and it may be the larger part) always comes from our own mind.

The fact that the brain is the one immediate bodily condition of the mental operations is indeed so universally admitted nowadays that I need spend no more time in illustrating it, but will simply postulate it and pass on.

William James,
The Principals of Psychology,
Volume I, 1890, Foreword

The patients have, at first at least, no real understanding of the gravity of the disorder...

To all representations of the incomprehensibility and morbidity of their conduct the patients give as answers explanations which say nothing.

Emil Kraeplin
Manic-Depressive Insanity and Paranoia, 1919, pg.151

Chapter 1
Overview

This book is divided into four sections. The first provides vital information on the nature and scope of the problem you are about to tackle. Some readers may be tempted to skip this section and go directly to Chapter 5, where I introduce you to four steps that will help you "convince" the mentally ill person you are worried about to accept medication and other forms of treatment. Or, if the situation is more urgent, you may want to turn directly to Chapter 10, where I provide a practical guide explaining when and how you can secure "assisted treatment" (inpatient or outpatient commitment). In my mind, skipping ahead would be an appropriate use of this book. If you do this, however, I strongly urge you to go back after things have settled down and read the three chapters that make up Part I.

It's difficult to maintain your resolve when you are dealing with someone who wants no part of what you are offering.

The chapters in Part I are vital for several reasons. All three discuss new research that will help you understand what you are up against and how best to approach the problem. In Chapter 2 you will learn about the scope of the problem and the reason you should not take it personally or blame the person who is mentally ill for refusing help. Chapter 3 describes research that explains why medication (pharmacological treatment) is so vital for the health, safety, and general well-being of persons with serious mental illness. What you will learn will increase your desire to deal with the problem of poor insight into illness and medication refusal. It's difficult to maintain your resolve when you are dealing with someone who wants no part of what you are offering. Knowing just how vital treatment is will help you to persevere.

The purpose of this section of the book is to bring you up-to-date on scientific advances, and by doing so, make you more effective at helping.

"Poor insight," as described in this book, is a condition that renders seriously mentally ill people incapable of understanding that they're sick, have symptoms, and would benefit from treatment. Chapter 4 provides an overview of the new research on poor insight which is, not surprisingly, a major cause of refusal to take medication. The purpose of this section of the book is to bring you up-to-date on scientific advances, and by doing so, make you more effective at helping. More specifically, in this Chapter I tell you about the brain dysfunction that underlies severe cases of poor insight to emphasize that the only enemy you have to deal with is the illness. Too often, people with these disorders feel that we (I am speaking both as a therapist and as a family member now) are their enemies. From their perspective we are adversaries and detractors - definitely not allies. Meanwhile, we scratch our heads and wonder why they seem unable, or unwilling, to accept the help we offer. In this context it is not surprising that the relationship often becomes adversarial.

The only enemy you have to deal with is the illness.

If, after reading this chapter, you have further questions about the research. Chapter 14 and the appendix list other sources of information. Also, on the ***www.VidaPress.com*** web site I will answer ongoing questions you may have and provide updates on the relevant research.

Countless times following lectures I have given to professional and lay audiences (family members and consumers/patients) audience members have told me that knowledge of the new research has helped to alleviate guilt.

Just as often I am told that this information helps to diminish blame and anger directed toward the mentally ill person who is refusing help. If you are feeling angry and blaming the person you are trying to help (common and natural feelings) you will be much less effective in what you are trying to accomplish. It will also make your task an unhappy adversarial endeavor rather than a positive collaboration.

Once you know the nature of the problem and why you urgently need to address it, you will be better prepared for Part II of the book. Chapter 5 describes a new approach to dealing with poor insight and treatment

If my previous experience and the published research are any indication, chances are very good that you can make a very positive difference.

refusal that is based on scientific studies and on nearly twenty years of personal and professional experience. Chapters 6, 7, 8, and 9 give a step-by-step strategy for improving medication adherence and those aspects of insight that are linked to it. The techniques you will learn are not only informed by the research on insight and medication adherence you will have read about in chapters 2 and 3, but also based on the results of recent *placebo controlled studies* of a new short-term psychotherapy, and on my clinical experience working with patients and families and with supervising other therapists. Obviously I can't guarantee the strategy I give will definitely raise the level of insight and eliminate medication refusal in the person you're concerned about, but I can promise you that if you faithfully follow the guidelines I give, they will help. If my previous experience and the published research are any indication, chances are very good that you can make a very positive difference.

During the time you are working on the problem, you may face the difficult dilemma of countless other family members and therapists: whether or not to force medicate using the psychiatric commitment laws in your state. This can sometimes be a vital part of the treatment process. But it is most effective when it is done in such a way as to ulti-

In this section, you will not only learn the nuts and bolts of how to seek a commitment to the hospital, but also how to deal with the difficult feelings this intervention raises for everyone involved.

mately strengthen your alliance with the mentally ill person rather than destroy it. Part III of this book focuses on the question of when to "commit or not commit" someone to hospital or outpatient treatment[1] against their will. In this section, you will not only learn the nuts and bolts of how to seek a commitment to the hospital, but also how to deal with the difficult feelings this intervention raises for everyone involved. My main goal is to show you ways to deal with the accusations of betrayal you will likely encounter, the guilt you may feel, and, most importantly, how to use such instances to build trust and a sense of teamwork with the very person you forced into treatment.

Too often treatment is crisis-driven and hence short-sighted. What happens after discharge from the hospital, or after you have achieved success in raising the level of insight and medication adherence is the focus of Part IV. Chapter 13 explains how you can preserve the trust and gains you have achieved, even during episodes of the illness. You will also learn from some of the more common mistakes others have made. A list of resources you can use to learn more about mental illness, medication, new research, and other relevant information is given in Chapter 14. The appendices I give will help you in a number of ways: by providing a checklist for you to better understand your loved one's experience of their illness and treatment, a list of professional and consumer oriented organizations that can be of help, where to find free information on medications and side effects, recommendations for further reading, a glossary of terms, and

---

1. Some states have outpatient commitment laws. In select cases these laws allow family members and clinicians to seek a court order to medicate the mentally ill person against their will without requiring hospitalization.

information on a web site available from Vida Press that is devoted exclusively to the problem of poor insight and medication refusal.

Throughout this book, I encourage family members who are not involved with one of the family and consumer organizations I list to get involved. There are many reasons to do so, not the least of which is to feel less alone and more supported in your quest to better the life of your mentally ill relative. These organizations will also help you to feel less ashamed and embarrassed about having a mentally ill person in your family. These feelings are unwarranted, and will only hinder you in your attempts to help your loved one.

It was only last year that Anna-Lisa, who contributed to this book, became involved with the National Alliance for the Mentally Ill and other family/consumer organizations. Her mother, who had been variably diagnosed with schizophrenia and bipolar disorder, became famous after her illness tricked her into believing that she was married to the television talk show host David

Whether you are a mental health professional or a family member, this book will help to dispel the despair that sometimes makes you want to turn your head and look the other way and give you renewed hope you can make a big difference.

Letterman. The common impulse to keep mental illness a family secret was amplified a hundred-fold when her mother became the butt of jokes on national television. For many years Anna-Lisa believed she was the only person in the world trying to cope with a mentally ill parent. This isolation from others with more private, but very similar, stories only added to her experience of embarrassment and shame. It was only after her mother's suicide that she discovered and participated in these organizations. She has told me countless times that she wished she had known about such organizations and gotten involved years ago. She believes that if she had, her mother's illness would have had less of a negative impact on her own life and that perhaps she would have been better able to help. It took me even longer than it took Anna-Lisa. For too many years I was ashamed about my brother who has schizophrenia.

> *It is ironic and sad that the instinct not to talk about family problems keeps many of us away from the support and information we need to solve those problems.*

Despite knowing that he suffered from a brain disorder and that I had nothing to feel ashamed about, I avoided such organizations and kept his illness a secret from my colleagues. It was only after talking with people like myself that my belief that I should not feel ashamed became a reality. So I would understand if you don't feel that you are ready to attend any kind of meeting or conference about mental illness. It is ironic and sad that the instinct not to talk about family problems keeps many of us away from the support and information we need to solve those problems. However, you can benefit from such organizations even if you still feel hesitant about getting involved. You don't have to attend a single meeting to subscribe to newsletters and to request other literature offered by these groups. Anna-Lisa and I have learned much from these organizations and have found great comfort in knowing that there are many other families like ours and, that there are forces at work to change mental health laws, fund research, and improve treatments.

For therapists who read this book, I aim to give you hope you can reach your patients/clients with serious mental illness who don't think they're ill and refuse your help. Whether you are a mental health professional or a family member, this book will help to dispel the despair that sometimes makes you want to turn your head and look the other way and give you renewed hope you can make a big difference.

Part I

Why they Deny having an Illness and Refuse Help

Chapter 2
You Have More Company than You Know

"My brother is so ill. He's refused to take the medication. We've tried to talk him into it," said April Callahan, sister of Russel Weston who is charged with having shot two guards at the U.S. Capitol. "He just wouldn't do it," added his mother, Arbah Weston. "What are we going to do with a 41-year-old man? You can't throw him in the car."source AP wire July 26, 1998.

"After Jeff's last manic episode I thought he'd finally realized he needed to stay on the Lithium. When he was sick he had these fantastic ideas that he said would make us millions but all that happened was he ran up $21,000 in debt. Once he was back in his right mind, he was mortified and so angry with himself. So I thought 'It's worth our savings if he finally learned he needs this medication.' But last week he stopped taking his Lithium. He says he's better now and doesn't need it anymore! I am really scared and don't know what to do." Julia a forty-year-old mother of two, as told to the author.

"My mother wanted us to camp out on his land for two weeks to try and convince him to get help. As far as he was concerned we had the problem, not him." David Kaczynski, brother of the confessed 'Unabomber' Ted Kaczynski, as told to the author.

"I remembered how she looked and how she held me and how much I loved her and how we could be happy together, and then there was the sick person [who] broke into David Letterman's house. At that point, that wasn't my mother. That was her illness. She had an aversion to treatment and to admitting that she had a problem. Anna-Lisa Johanson, as told to the author.

Whenever the stories of families of the seriously mentally ill reach our national consciousness, it has been in the context of "newsworthy" tragedies. Reluctantly, we see ourselves and our loved ones in the newspaper headlines that both inform and mislead the general public. Julia's predicament, which was never the focus of any news story, highlights a problem encountered by millions of families whose names never appear in the newspapers. It is a far more common story than violence and suicide. Just like the infamous examples I have given, her loved one does not think he is ill and does not want to take medication.

Far more common than the tragedies that make headlines are the those that test the bonds of family and the moral resolve of therapists who are trusted with the care of our loved ones.

Many people with serious mental illnesses, such as manic-depression and schizophrenia, think of their illness as something that comes and goes. For a short time, Jeff acknowledged he had an illness and took the medication prescribed for it. But after things got better, he decided he didn't need to keep taking the lithium. For Jeff, lithium was for his mental illness like antibiotics are for an infection. When the bottle is empty, you are cured. In reality, the better comparison is that lithium is for manic depression like insulin is for diabetes, a chemical that is needed every day to prevent a relapse or worsening of the illness. Even though Jeff was erratic with his medication, he was still a step ahead of the game. Many people with serious mental illness have never acknowledged that they're ill and refuse to take medication even once.

David Kaczynski told me that he had received countless letters from family members of persons with serious mental illness who expressed their condolences and support for what his family was going through. Like David and his mother, they also were worried about loved one's who "denied" being ill and refused to get help. We see our own situation in that of the Kaczynski and Weston families.

We've just been luckier, or so it seems.

Far more common than the tragedies that make headlines are the those that test the bonds of family and the moral resolve of therapists who are trusted with the care of our loved ones. When once again a bottle of medication is found in the trash bin, when we are told to mind our own business, that we are the only one who has a problem, when yet another doctor's appointment is missed, we all come one step closer to throwing our hands up in despair. Sometimes, whether or not we walk away, our *loved ones*[2] do. They disappear for hours, days, weeks and even years. Some reach the headlines anonymously when they join the ranks of the homeless. That used to be my biggest fear. My brother Henry was prone to disappearing for days and even hitch-hiking cross country. Anna-Lisa's mother also frequently disappeared, but for weeks and months at a time. The only information she had on her mother's whereabouts came from newspapers, tabloid magazines and from acquaintances who saw her hitch-hiking or at a truck stop.

There are over five million people in the United States with schizophrenia, psychotic depression, and manic-depression. You probably already had some idea of how widespread these illnesses are, but did you ever stop and think about how many of *us*[3] there are? If we only count the

---

2. Since this book is written for the reader who is trying to help someone with a serious mental illness, there are many terms I could use (consumer, family member, patient, relative, client, etc.). To avoid cumbersome language I will use the terms "loved one," "family member," or "relative," from this point forward. Readers who are mental health care providers should substitute "patient," "client," or "consumer" (whatever the preference), for the familial reference.

3. Here, I am speaking as one family member to another. But I am also a therapist who has been entrusted with the care of people with serious mental disorders. I know that the frustration and despair created by denial of illness and treatment refusal are also very real for those of us in the helping professions. The common divide between the doctor and the patient's family has no place in this book or in the treatment of persons with psychotic disorders. In this spirit of collaboration, I share the valuable lessons I have learned about denial and treatment refusal.

Most studies find that about one half of the people with serious mental illness don't take their medication. The most common reason is poor insight into illness.

parents of these individuals, there are twice that number of family members! Add just one sibling or offspring, and the number becomes truly staggering. More to the point, you probably never realized that for more than half of us, the quotes I gave above hit very close to home. The results of recent studies are unequivocal, millions of people with these disorders don't believe they're ill and refuse to take the medications that have been prescribed for them.

In the past ten years, there has been an explosion of research on the problem of poor insight in psychotic disorders. Despite the fact that clinicians have always shown an interest in the problem, surprisingly few studies had been done until very recently. In the next chapter, you will learn why so much progress has been made in so short a time. You will learn more about exactly what we have learned and how that knowledge can help you. For now, it is important that you know that poor insight into illness is as common as the refusal to accept treatment. Most studies find that about half of the people with serious mental illness don't take their medication. The most common reason is poor insight.

My colleagues and I were part of a group of researchers that studied over 400 patients with psychotic disorders from all over the United States. This "field trial" study for psychotic disorders was conducted as part of our participation in the revision of the Diagnostic and Statistical Manual for Mental Disorders conducted by the American Psychiatric Association. We measured a wide range of symptoms, including insight into different aspects of the illness and treatment. We hoped to learn how frequently people with a mental disorder did not realize they were ill. Our results showed that nearly 60% of the patients with schizophrenia, about 25% of those with schizoaffective disorder, and near- ly 50% of subjects with manic depression, were essentially unaware of being ill. In other words, when asked whether they had any mental, psychiatric, or emotional problems, they answered "no." Usually the "no" was emphatic and followed by sometimes bizarre explanations as to why they were in the hospital. Their explanations as to why they were inpatients on a psychiatric ward ranged from "because my parents brought me here" to more bizarre beliefs such as "I'm just here for a general physical." These individuals were unlike the majority of patients with depression and anxiety disorders who actively seek treatment because they feel badly. Instead, these individuals seemed unaware of having any problems whatsoever, outside of feeling victimized by their families and doctors.

A large percentage were also not aware of the various signs of the illness that they "suffered" from, despite the fact that everyone around them could recognize the symptoms readily (e.g., *disordered speech, disorganized behaviors, hallucinations, negative symptoms*, etc.). Or if they were aware of the signs of illness, or aware that some of their beliefs, perceptions and behaviors were very odd, they didn't believe they were symptoms of an illness. If you step back and think about some discussions you might have had with your loved one, the degree of "denial"[4] is really astounding.

Let's look at an example from a former patient of mine to illustrate how deep the denial can be. But don't despair, I also chose this example because, as you will learn in later chapters, I was able to help this man develop insight into some key aspects of the illness. This awareness ultimately enabled him[5] to accept medicine and to become an active

---

4. The term denial suggests that the person is being defensive and that poor insight into the illness is an act of will. After the third chapter I will rarely use the term again. By the time you finish reading this book, if not by the end of chapter 3, I hope to have convinced you that referring to the problem as "denial" is usually incorrect as the problem typically stems from a deficit in self-awareness that is caused by brain dysfunction, not defensiveness.

5. Mental illness affects men and women, consequently, throughout this book I alternate between the masculine and feminine pronouns.

participant in the treatment that was being offered. And, not surprisingly, the endless stream of conflicts with his family over his refusal to stay in treatment came to an end.

Matt

Matt is twenty-six-years-old, single, and lives alone with his parents. He was diagnosed with schizoaffective disorder six years ago when he was first troubled by grandiose and paranoid delusions (e.g., he thought he was a special messenger from God, knew President Clinton personally, and he worried that the CIA was trying to kill him). He had disorganized speech, bizarre behaviors (e.g. wearing broken earphones that had been wrapped in aluminum foil). He was hearing voices. Actually, to be more accurate he was remarkably untroubled by his obvious signs of illness. On the other hand, these unambiguous signs of mental illness gravely troubled his family, friends, fellow students, and even neighbors. Since the time when he first became ill, he had been hospitalized on four occasions.

At the time of the interview you are about to read, he had voluntarily signed himself into our Schizophrenia Research Ward at Columbia University in New York City. He came to us from a city hospital where he had been receiving medication for one month. However, in that instance he was absolutely not a willing participant in the treatment. In fact, he was brought to that hospital's emergency room by the police after his mother called 911.

No one knows for certain, but at least six weeks prior to that night Matt had stopped taking his medications. On the night his mother phoned the police, the paranoia that had been brewing for days boiled over. Matt began to scream at his mother. He accused her of interfering with his mission from God. Matt believed that God had chosen him as his special messenger to world leaders, and he was paranoid that his mother was trying to interfere with his delivery of a vital message to President Clinton. His speech was disorganized. He was hearing voices. In recent days he had been frantically writing letters to President Clinton and trying to place phone calls to the White House. More frightening to his mother: He was hearing God's voice telling him to lock her in the closet.

At the time of my interview on the Schizophrenia Research Unit, nearly all of his symptoms, except the *delusions,* had shown significant improvement. Although he still believed he was God's messenger and that the CIA was trying to kill him, he felt less urgency about these ideas and less worried about his safety. In fact, despite his obviously poor insight into the illness, he was about to be discharged to his parents' home with a referral to an outpatient treatment program. I started the interview by asking Matt to tell me how he came to be in the hospital.

"I think it was... I don't know the exact terms. It wasn't identified to me as of yet. I think they brought me here for a general physical. They wanted to know was I drinking, had I been smoking. I told the police that there wasn't any drinking, no smoking. It was just a mild argument we had and I believe that my mother had more seniority over what was going on. So they took me to the clinic to have the doctor make the determination of how well off I am."

Although Matt's speech is somewhat tangential and a touch idiosyncratic I caught the geste of what he was trying to tell me and asked "So when you were having an argument with your mother someone called the police." He nodded. "Was it your mother?"

"I think so."

"Why did your mother call the police?"

"I don't know. She wanted me to go to the hospital."

"Why did your mother want you to come here?"

"She said she didn't really want me to go to the hospital in the event that an argument like that took place, because we were discussing my use of the telephone."

"I am a little confused by what you just said." I admitted "Why did she want you to go to a hospital?"

"We were arguing and I think she thought I was sick and needed to be checked out."

"Were you sick?"

"No. We were just arguing."

"So the police brought you to the hospital."

"That's right."

"Why did the people at the hospital admit you?"

"They didn't say. A real friendly guy was there, he said 'don't worry you're going to be here for a while and I'd like you to get your thoughts together,' and I've been in the hospital ever since."

"Yes. But that was in the emergency room. What kind of a ward did you go to?"

"I went to a psychiatric ward upstairs. They removed me of my clothes and they told me I was going to stay there for a while."

"But why a psychiatric ward?"

"I think that's all they have available now because of the heavy drug and alcohol use. They may not be receiving aid for a general check-up clinic."

"Matt, now I am confused. Are you saying the doctors at the City hospital admitted you to a psychiatric ward for a general physical?"

"That's right," he answered deadpan as if there was nothing unusual or upsetting about his perception of his circumstance.

"So do you see yourself as someone who didn't need to be in a psychiatric ward?" I paused and then added "Do you see yourself as someone without psychiatric or emotional problems of any sort?"

"That's right. But they put me through the emotional tests because of the two party system. They asked me to cooperate. So I've been pretty much cooperating. Some of it is against my will but I can cooperate."

"You didn't want to stay. Is that right?"

"Right."

"Why did you stay?"

"I had to because of the judge, he committed me for a month."

"But after the month was up you decided to come here, to the Schizophrenia Research Ward. Yes?"

"Right."

"But you feel there is nothing wrong with you?"

"That's right. My mother wanted me to come, but there's nothing wrong with me."

To say that Matt has poor insight into his illness is an understatement. It does not do justice to the strangeness of the beliefs he has about what is happening to him. Matt believes that police officers restrained him and brought him to the hospital at the request of his mother simply because she had more seniority than him. And that an emergency room physician admitted him to a psychiatric ward for one month simply to get a "general physical." And what can we make of the blasé attitude he has while he describes these terrible injustices. Handcuffed by the police, brought to a hospital and incarcerated against his will for a month and he doesn't threaten lawsuits or scream bloody murder? Many patients with these illnesses do exactly that, while others have the remarkable lack of distress that Matt shows.

What is going on here? Is it that Matt was embarrassed by his mental illness and didn't want to reveal the truth to me? That is possible, except wouldn't a less bizarre explanation be more convincing? More important, Matt already knew that I was well aware of all the details of his hospitalization. I was the doctor assigned to his care!

You will read more of my conversation with Matt in the pages ahead. You might have guessed from what you have already learned that he was also unaware that the voices he heard were unusual. He accepted them as if they were nothing out of the ordinary and certainly nothing to be concerned about.

Imagine if *you* suddenly started hearing voices when no one was in the room. What would you do? More likely than not, most people who experience false perceptions such as these become worried and if the hallucinations occur more than a couple of times they rush to a doctor. I know. I have worked in neurological clinics with such people. Sometimes hallucinations are among the first symptoms of a brain tumor. But why do some people worry when they hallucinate and others don't? Is it simply denial? Is it that some people are more able to accept that they have problems while others are too frightened, proud or stubborn? Or is there some other explanation?

At this level, poor insight into having an illness and into the benefits of treatment is clearly another symptom of the disorder, and has nothing to do with being defensive or stubborn.

Chances are very good that Matt was not in denial. Instead, our research and that of other clinical scientists tells us that Matt had at least one more symptom, other than thought disorder, that had not been helped by the medicine he was given. His bizarre explanations for why he was in a psychiatric hospital (for a general physical and because all the other wards were filled with drug-addicted patients) and his failure to see that he was ill and could benefit from medicine, was not stemming from denial or pridefulness. At this level, poor insight into having an illness and into the benefits of treatment is clearly another symptom of the disorder. It has nothing to do with being defensive or stubborn. Indeed, the research you will read about in Chapter 3 explains how this type of poor insight is more readily understood as one of the *neurocognitive deficits,* or symptoms of a brain dysfunction, that are commonly associated with these disorders. This is very important information because only when you understand the causes of poor insight can you be effective at dealing with the refusal to take medication that it creates. The first step in that understanding is to correct some common misconceptions about insight that you may have.

Whether in the context of supervising psychiatrists, psychologists, social workers or nurses, I keep running into some extremely dangerous myths that have survived the era when psychoanalysis was thought to be the treatment of choice for psychotic disorders. One myth frequently shared by family members is: "When you're that sick, insight could kill you." Many people believe it would be better to just let sleeping dogs lie. If someone like Matt developed insight into the fact that he is gravely ill he would probably become demoralized, if not suicidal.

Is there such a thing as too much insight? Here again we can turn to some new research to guide us. What you will learn in the next

When you're that sick, insight could kill you.

chapter is that its not a question of quantity but of quality. In other words, there is good insight and bad insight. The good kind increases participation in treatment and adherence to medication, while the bad kind can lead to demoralization and suicide. The main lesson you will learn is that when you avoid dealing with poor insight and refusal to take medication, the problems they cause not only don't go away, but usually worsen. The most obvious consequences of avoiding the problem are *revolving door admissions* to the hospital. Sadly, in the context of the headlines I referred to earlier, repeated hospitalizations and the disruptions they cause are also among the least tragic.

Notes:

Chapter 3

Let Sleeping Dogs Lie?

"Far better is it to dare mighty things, to win glorious triumphs, even though checkered by failure, than to take up ranks with those poor spirits who neither enjoy much nor suffer much, for they live in that grey twilight that knows neither victory nor defeat." Theodore Roosevelt

I wouldn't blame you if you were sometimes tempted to let the problem slide. Whether you are family, friend, or therapist, eventually you get tired of being told, "there's nothing wrong with me, I don't need help." Often we feel so helpless.

As Russell Weston's mother remarked in an interview after her son shot and killed two U.S. Capitol Police Officers, "What are we going to do with a 41-year-old man? You can't throw him in the car, and drive him to the doctor". I wouldn't be surprised if she and her husband wished they had done exactly that, or they had involuntarily committed their son to a hospital. But these things are much easier said than done. In Part III of this book, you will learn about forced treatment (a.k.a. assisted treatment). Still, the decision whether to commit someone or not is very personal, much like your choice to read this book and learn how to deal with denial and refusal to accept treatment. To attack the problem, you must have hope that your efforts will make a difference. Otherwise it's much easier to let events unfold as they may. Who hasn't thought that sooner or later, another hospitalization will end the current crisis. And, when there is no crisis, the temptation to "let sleeping dogs lie," is even greater.

Whenever things are calm and a mentally ill family

member has stopped taking her medication, we can't help but want to back off a little. This is especially true when faced with personal accusations. For example, Vicky, a forty-five-year-old mother of two with manic depression told her worried husband, "I'm not sick anymore. I am not the one with the problem, You're the one with the problem! Get off my back and stop trying to control me!" And then there is the therapist or family member who suspects, but can't prove, that a loved one has been throwing out medications. We often back off because we don't want a negative confrontation to further weaken whatever trust we have. Later, I will explain how you don't have to back off and what you can do to build trust so you can persuade a loved one to stay in treatment. But first, I need to debunk the myth that in cases of serious mental illness it is sometimes better to "let sleeping dogs lie."

Of course you could simply ignore the problem when things are going well. But what happens when you wait for events to unfold or if you never tackle the problem of poor insight into the illness?

Like many families and therapists, we are tempted to simply ignore the problems of poor insight and medication adherence when a family member is stable and things are generally going well. We sit back and wait for the next crisis to force the issue or hope (our own form of denial) that the disease has gone away. Anna-Lisa spent many years trying to cover up her mother's illness whenever it flared up again. It was much easier to pretend that the situation was not as bad as it appeared because facing the reality of the illness felt intimidating and hopeless. But what happens when we wait for events to unfold and never tackle the problem of poor insight into the illness?

The new research answers these questions. Research shows that getting the seriously mentally ill into treatment early, and keeping them there, is very important. It has always been obvious that consistent supervision and treatment help to prevent suicide, violence, homelessness, and reckless behaviors. What had not been clear until recently is the very positive effect that early and consistent treatment has on the course of the ill-

> *Some scientists have gone so far as to argue that psychotic episodes are toxic to the brain.*

ness and the hope of recovery. Recent studies also make it clear that increasing particular aspects of insight into illness is also vital. Understanding this research will help you to make an informed decision about what to do. If you decide to tackle the problem of poor insight and make facilitating consistent involvement in treatment your goal, the following information will help you keep your resolve.

Why We Can't Let Sleeping Dogs Lie

Whenever someone with serious mental illness has another episode, the long term prognosis worsens, according to new research. Some scientists have gone so far as to argue that psychotic episodes[6] are toxic to the brain. The idea here is that brain cells are altered or die during and immediately following an episode of psychosis. As of yet there is no definitive evidence for this idea, but there is a good deal of indirect support coming from long-term studies of the seriously mentally ill.

In a landmark study conducted at the Hillside Hospital in Queens, New York, researchers found those schizophrenia patients that received treatment early and consistently had much better outcomes. The results of the study indicate that whenever antipsychotic drugs are given shortly after the illness first emerges and subsequent psychotic episodes are treated quickly to shorten their duration, future response to

6.   Most people refer to psychotic episodes as 'nervous breakdowns.' But the term nervous breakdown is sometimes used to indicate conditions other than psychosis. An episode of psychosis specifically involves hallucinations, delusions, and/or extremely disorganized thoughts and behavior.

treatment and prognosis is greatly improved.

Similar results were found in a follow-up study, involving 276 young, seriously mentally ill persons. Researchers studied these patients during an episode of psychosis and then stayed in contact with them for up to seven-and-one-half years. Subjects who had more psychotic episodes during the early stages of the study did much worse years later. Once again, the results strongly suggest that by limiting the number of full-blown episodes of psychosis and intervening early whenever the illness does flair up, patients are higher functioning and less ill later in life.

Finally, in a fifteen-year follow up study of 82 patients with schizophrenia, researchers found that delays in mental-health treatment and longer periods of psychosis led to a worse prognosis over the long run. This study is especially informative because patients were entered into the research during their very first episode of illness.

The studies just described are but a few examples of the growing body of evidence supporting early intervention in patients with schizophrenia who refuse to take medication. Furthermore, research indicates that the same holds true for other serious mental illnesses. For example, clinical depression with, or without, psychosis.

In the book *When Someone You Love is Depressed: How to help your loved one without losing yourself,* my co-author Dr. Laura Rosen and I review the research on treatment of depression. Most studies find that people with episodes of clinical depression that are not treated (i.e., they "ride the depression out") have a much worse course of illness and more frequent bouts of depression later in life.

Research shows that people with bipolar disorder, or manic depression, also do more poorly when episodes of illness are not treated quickly and effectively. A more thorough description of this important research can be found in the first chapter of *Out of the Shadows: Confronting America's Mental Illness Crisis* by Dr. E. Fuller Torrey. Among the reasons Dr. Torrey cites for getting the seriously mentally ill medical attention are the following statistics:

- 2.2 million Americans with untreated severe mental illness;
- 150,000 of them are homeless;
- 159,000 incarcerated for crimes committed while unmedicated.

He argues that homelessness, incarceration, episodes of violence, and premature death are not necessary because we know what to do, but fail to do it for economic, legal, and ideological reasons. In particular, he cites our hesitation as a society to infringe on the individual rights and freedoms of our fellow citizens as a major obstacle to providing the seriously mentally ill with the medical treatment they need. The issue he takes on is largely beyond the scope of this book, but the case he makes for getting people with serious mental illness into treatment and for finding ways to help them become active participants in their own care is directly relevant. I encourage you to read this book, especially if, by the end of this chapter, you still have doubts about the tremendously positive impact you will have when you help someone with serious mental illness accept treatment.

For our purposes, the three studies described above make the point that when we ignore the problem it not only doesn't go away, it gets worse. We must address the twin problems of poor insight and medication refusal if we want our loved one to have the best possible chance of recovery. In many ways, medication refusal can be seen as a symptom of the underlying problem of poor insight. The good news is that in recent years scientists have learned a lot about the nature and causes of poor insight in serious mental disorders. The research suggests a focus and specific methods for dealing with the problem. Unlike some advances in research, this is news you can use right now.

> *We must address the twin problems of poor insight and medication refusal if we want our loved one to have the best possible chance of recovery.*

Myths and Facts about Insight

The best place to begin is to dispel some myths that have been revealed by recent research. One of the most common myths is that having poor insight is usually a good thing. Many times I have participated in clinical conferences when a well meaning mental health professional said, "No wonder he's in denial: if he had insight he might kill himself!" I also used to think this way. However, the new research shows that insight is usually a very good thing, but, like most good things, only in moderation. In other words, insight into some aspects of the illness is usually beneficial, while other types of insight can sometimes be detrimental.

Research shows that awareness of the positive effects of medication can be more important to medication adherence than insight into the illness more generally.

In 1991, my colleagues at Columbia University and I published a paper in the National Institute of Mental Health's journal *Schizophrenia Bulletin* in which we proposed several guidelines for researchers interested in studying insight. The first guideline was that insight should be measured in all its complexity. When I use the term "insight" I am referring to much more than whether or not a mentally ill person can say, "yes, I am ill." There are different things one can have insight into and some types of awareness are more vital to recovery than others. For example, one can have insight into the fact that antipsychotic medication helps them to function in society without necessarily agreeing that they're mentally ill. Research shows that awareness of the positive effects of medication can be more important to medication adherence than insight into illness more generally. I have seen patients who are aware of some of their symptoms while unaware that the voices that they alone hear are a sign of illness. Meanwhile, others will say they're ill but don't believe they gain any benefit from taking medication despite objective evidence to the contrary. The guidelines we proposed nearly ten years ago are now widely accepted by the scientific community and the pace of research on the problem of poor insight has increased dramatically.

It is also important to recognize that insight is not an all or nothing phenomenon, as some people have complete insight into every aspect of their illness while others have only a glimmer. For example, Vicky had this to say when I interviewed her in the hospital shortly after her admission to receive treatment for a manic episode.

"I am emotionally unstable. I know I lose it sometimes and get too grandiose and I have to be careful when I get on a roll. But that's just because I am creative."

"Is that what your family thinks?" I asked, knowing that her husband practically dragged her into the hospital.

"My family thinks I'm a manic depressive and need to take lithium."

"What do you think?"

"It's possible that I do, but I don't know."

Even Matt showed a little bit of insight during the same interview you read excerpts from above when he told me: "Sometimes I get really paranoid. It's my nerves." A glimmer of insight is an open door to developing more.

Regardless of which aspects of insight are being measured, most studies find that the more aware a seriously mentally ill person is of their illness and of the benefits of treatment, the better the prognosis. Patients with better insight have shorter periods in a hospital and fewer hospitalizations overall. No one knows for sure why this is the case, but it's easy to imagine especially in light of studies showing that various kinds of insight into illness promote adherence to treatment. In the work conducted at our research center, we found that awareness of the beneficial effects of medication is one of the best predictors of adherence to medication. If you would like more details about these studies, have a look at the recommended readings listed in the back of this book, the section titled "research on insight" in the appendix, or log on to *www.VidaPress.com* for up-to-date information and resources.

Many people believe that side effects are the most

important reason why so many refuse to take their medication. In fact, the research shows that it is awareness of the illness and of the beneficial effects of medication that is the most important predictor of reliable adherence to medication. Since this point has been made earlier and is a premise of this book, I will not belabor it here. However, it is worth noting that forms of treatment adherence other than medication are similarly affected by poor insight. For example, Dr. Paul Lysaker and Dr. Morris Bell of Yale University evaluated patients when stabilized and enrolled in an outpatient, work-rehabilitation program. Patients with schizophrenia and schizoaffective disorder with poor insight had very poor adherence to the psychosocial treatments (day hospital programs, occupational therapy, etc.) they had agreed to participate in, despite a stated desire to work. The researchers conclude that individuals with poor insight are likely to have more problems remaining in a course of treatment regardless of whether it involves drugs or psychotherapy.

Patients with poor insight while in crisis generally have lower levels of insight even when stable.

Another myth is that the sicker one is the worse the insight. Actually, most studies find that this is not true. If left unattended, the level of insight is generally stable in most patients. Patients with poor insight while in crisis generally have lower levels of insight even when stable. If you are reading this book, then likely the person you are concerned about fits this category. Whether their symptoms are under control or not, they persist in the belief that they really don't need medication. They may acknowledge that they were sick in the past, but not now.

In a study conducted by Dr. Joseph McEvoy and his colleagues at Duke University, patients with schizophrenia were followed from two-and-a-half, to three-and-a-half, years after discharge from the hospital. Although symptoms of psychosis improved in nearly all of the patients over the course of the hospitalization, patients who had been involuntarily committed to the hospital did not show any improvement in level of insight into the illness. Furthermore, the low level of insight persisted throughout the follow-up period. Not surprisingly, these same patients were more likely to be involuntarily committed over the course of follow-up. The authors conclude that an inability to see oneself as ill seems to be a persistent trait in some patients with schizophrenia and one that leads to commitment.

The last myth to be debunked by the research concerns the idea that insight into illness when one is seriously mentally ill will almost always lead to demoralization, depression and suicidal thoughts. Suicide is a very serious problem in both

> *It wasn't insight or a lessening of her delusions that led to her suicide; it was the fact that her mother did not receive adequate follow-up treatment.*

depression and schizophrenia. Estimates are that as many as one out of every ten persons with schizophrenia will kill themselves. I was taught, like most clinicians, that poor insight in patients with chronic mental illness, though problematic for treatment adherence, may be a godsend with respect to suicide. The assumption is that patients who don't believe that they're ill are less likely to be depressed and suicidal. Alternatively, those patients who recognize and acknowledge the illness will be more suicidal. In fact, in a study my colleagues and I conducted, we found that contrary to clinical lore, awareness of having an illness was not associated with increased suicidal thoughts or behavior. This study suggests that poor insight into having an illness is not a protective factor, as previously believed, and argues against the strategy of leaving such patients who are unaware of their illness and refuse treatment to fend for themselves.

During my graduate training I also learned that when grandiose delusions (e.g., I am married to someone rich and famous) are successfully treated the risk of suicide increases. When Anna-Lisa's mother committed suicide, it was following a prolonged involuntary hospitalization during which she was medicated and her symptoms improved somewhat. Anna-Lisa and her mother's close friends believed that she committed suicide because the medication had caused her to lose the fantasy world that had been created by her delusions. In other words, when confronted with the reality that she was not the person her illness led her to believe she was, she couldn't bear it. This is a terrible and all too common myth. It wasn't insight or a lessening of her delusions that led to her suicide; it was the fact that her mother did not receive adequate follow-up treatment. She was not working closely with a doctor or therapist that she trusted. Had there been someone to help guide her through her new found grasp on reality, it is unlikely that she would have lost hope and taken her own life. The need for proper follow-up with a trusted mental health professional can't be over-emphasized.

Summary

The relevant facts revealed by the research are that higher levels of insight into illness predict:

- reliable and consistent adherence to medication
- fewer hospitalizations
- shorter hospital stays
- fewer commitments to the hospital
- active involvement in all aspects of treatment

The research also demonstrates the value of examining the various aspects of insight independently. Having done this, we now know that insight into having an illness generally is far less important than insight into certain early warning signs of the illness and of the beneficial effects of treatment. It is these two aspects of insight that the research, and my own clinical experience, suggest are key to increasing adherence to treatment.

In order to help your loved one increase their awareness of certain symptoms and of the positive effects of treatment, you will need to first understand the root of the problem. I have summarized additional research on this topic in the appendix. The research described in the appendix and in the next chapter suggests that poor insight in people with serious mental illness usually has little if anything to do with being defensive, stubborn, uneducated, uncooperative or simply difficult.

Notes:

Chapter 4
Knowing the Enemy

"This is not surprising, since the brain, the same organ we use to think about ourselves and assess our needs, is the same organ that is affected in schizophrenia and bipolar disorder" E. Fuller Torrey, et. al., commenting on the high prevalence of poor insight in the seriously mentally ill. (Schizophrenia and Manic Depressive Disorder, 1996, page 27)

Sitting around the table with me were two nurses, a therapy aid, a social worker and a psychiatrist. We were in the middle of our weekly clinical team meeting, discussing whether or not we thought Matt was well enough to be discharged from the hospital.

"His symptoms have vastly improved," began Maria, his primary nurse. "The hallucinations have responded to the medication, he's calmer and no longer paranoid."

"Both his mother and father are ready to have him come home again," added Cynthia, Matt's social worker, "and Dr. Remmers has agreed to see him as an outpatient."

"Sounds like we've got all our ducks lined up in a row," the team leader, Dr. Preston said, capping the discussion and scribbling a note in Matt's medical chart.

"Only one thing troubles me," Cynthia interjected hesitantly, "I don't think he's going to follow through with the treatment plan. He still doesn't think there's anything wrong with him."

"He's taking his medication," I observed.

"For now. But he's really stubborn and so defensive. I don't think that will last more than a week or two after he hits the sidewalk." I had to agree with Cynthia's prediction. But I didn't share her view as to *why* he wouldn't take his medication on the outside.

"What makes you say he's defensive?," I couldn't help but ask.

Nearly everyone around the table burst into laughter, thinking I was being facetious.

"No, really. I am serious."

The resident assigned to the case, Dr. Brian Greene, jumped into the discussion "Well, he doesn't think there is anything wrong with him. As far as Matt's concerned the only reason he is here is because his mother forced him into it. The man is full of pride and just plain stubborn. Don't get me wrong, I like him, but I don't think there is anything else we can do for him as long as he is in denial. No one's going to convince him that he's sick. He's just going to have to learn the lesson the hard way. He'll be back before he knows what hit him."

Asked about what his plans were after being discharged from yet another hospital- ization, he ritually answered, "All I need to do is get a job, there's nothing wrong with me."

Dr. Preston, recogniz- ing that Matt's discharge was a forgone conclusion, ended the discussion saying "You are probably right about that and about the fact that there is nothing more we can offer him here. When he's ready to stop denying his problems, we can help. Until then, our hands are tied. Brian, you're meeting with Matt and his par- ents at 3 o'clock to go over the plan. Any questions?" After a moments silence Matt's medical chart was passed around the table for each of us to sign off on the discharge plan.

During the first few years of my brother's illness, before I went to graduate school to become a clinical psychologist, I often thought he was being immature and stubborn. Asked about what his plans were after being discharged from yet another hospitalization, he ritually answered, "All I need to do is get a job, there's nothing wrong with me." His other stock answer was, "I am going to get married." Both desires are natural and understandable, but unrealistic given his recent history, the severity of the illness and his refusal to accept treatment. Someday perhaps he would realize his desires, but it was very unlikely unless he was actively involved in the treatment recommended by his doctors.

It was exasperating talking to him about why he wasn't taking his medication. Having limited experience with the illness, the only reason for his adamant refusal that I could think of was that he was being stubborn, defensive, and to be frank, a pain in the rear. I was lucky that I only thought of my brother as being stubborn. Because, like many children of people with serious mental illness, Anna-Lisa often wondered if her mother didn't love her enough to want to get better. It took her mother's suicide to educate Anna-Lisa about what was really happening. And for myself, it was only after I started working in the field and had met many more people with serious mental illness that I stopped giving such theories much credence. It just never made sense to me that the pervasive unawareness and odd explanations given by people like Matt and my brother could be explained by an immature personality or a lack of love. But you don't have to take my word for it. Lets look at the research for a more objective answer to the question of what causes poor insight and refusal to accept treatment.

Research on the Causes of Poor Insight

I have considered three different causes of poor insight in the seriously mentally ill. It could stem from defensiveness. After all, it makes sense that someone who is seriously ill would be in denial about all the potential and promise for the future that had been taken by the disease. On the other hand, perhaps it's simply cultural or educational differences between the mentally ill person and the people who are trying to help them. Often times, differences in subculture and values are blamed. For example, Anna-Lisa always believed that her mother's poor insight wasn't denial so much as a preference for the interesting and fantastic world that her illness gave her. When she was symptomatic, the world was a magical place filled with adventures to be had and mysteries to explore. Anna-Lisa never wanted to question her mother's delusions because she feared that by talking about them, she might take them away and somehow cause her mother more pain. And finally, the third cause I have considered is that poor insight into illness stems from the same brain dysfunction responsible for other symptoms of the disorder.

Historically, psychoanalytic theories predominated to explain poor insight in schizophrenia. Although the literature is rich with numerous case studies that seem to suggest that poor insight stems from defensive denial, the question had never been tested in controlled studies until recently. Two of my doctoral students, Chrysoula Kasapis and Elizabeth Nelson, took different approaches to this question in their thesis research. Dr. Kasapis examined the overall level of defensiveness in the patients she studied, while Dr. Nelson looked at the issue of stigma. Both approaches to the question failed to find anything of significance. Highly defensive patients were generally no more likely to have poor insight than those with little or no defensiveness. Similarly, how stigmatizing patients perceived their symptoms had little effect on how much insight they had into their illness. Everyone gets defensive from time to time and some are more prone to denial than others. The same holds true for people with serious mental illness. However, everyday defensiveness is not responsible for the gross deficits in insight that are so common in these patients.

Cultural differences between the examiner and patient may also play a role, at times, in mislabeling someone as having poor insight. In other words, the patient may be well aware of most if not all aspects of his mental illness, however his sub-culture labels it something else. Consequently, he would not use this label to describe himself. Instead he might say, "I have a nervous problem," or in the case of religious beliefs such as those common to some Carribean countries, "I am possessed by evil spirits." The sub-culture of the afflicted person needs to be addressed in any study of insight.

Related to the issue of cultural influences, is the question of patient education. Has the patient ever been told that he or she has an illness? If so, have they been taught how to identify and label symptoms of the disorder? In my experience, most patients with poor insight have been told about the illness they have, yet either claim they haven't or, if they recall being told, adamantly disagree, claiming superior knowledge to that of the doctors making the diagnosis. We also evaluate the question of patient knowledge and education about the illness in our studies. It's ironic, but many patients with poor insight into their own illness are excellent at diagnosing the same illness in others! The answer to the question of whether half of all people with serious mental

> *It's ironic, but many patients with poor insight into their own illness are excellent at diagnosing the same illness in others!*

illness don't know they are ill because they have no information about the illness is actually obvious when you step back for a moment. If you had heartburn that was bad enough that a friend or relative convinced you to go see your family doctor, who then diagnosed the problem as heart disease and explained that the pain was angina, you would stop referring to the pain as heartburn and start calling it angina. You would then make an appointment with a cardiologist and cancel your next appointment with the gastroenterologist. Why do so many people with schizophrenia and bipolar disorder fail to do this? Why do they persist in calling their pain "heartburn" despite all evidence to the contrary?

A Concept of Self that is Stranded in Time

In our paper published in 1991, my colleagues and I proposed that poor insight in people with serious mental disorders is a consequence of, to coin a phrase, a broken brain. We came to believe that pervasive problems with insight and the accompanying illogical ideas offered to explain being hospitalized were stemming from neurological deficits. At that time, we hadn't yet considered a neurological hypothe-

The neuropsychological deficits have left their concept of self, their beliefs about what they can and cannot do, literally stranded in time.

sis to explain poor insight in bipolar disorder. But we felt that there was good reason to believe that what we were seeing in patients with schizophrenia was indeed a consequence of brain dysfunction rather than stubbornness, defensiveness or ignorance about mental illness in general. The brain circuitry responsible for recording and updating self concept is not working properly in such patients.

My self-concept includes, among other things, the following beliefs about my abilities: I can hold down a job, if I went back to school, I believe that I would be a competent student; I believe that I have the education and experience to be a therapist, and I am generally socially appropriate when I interact with others. What are some of the beliefs you hold about yourself and your abilities? Do you believe that you can hold down a job? What if I told you that you were wrong, that you are incapable of working and may never find employment unless you swallowed some pills I had for you. And, by the way, you will have to take these pills for a very long time, if not for the rest of your life. What would you say to that? Probably the same thing my brother once said to me when I told him he would never hold down a job again unless he took his medication faithfully, "You're out of your mind!" If I said this to you, you would likely think I was joking, and after I convinced you that I was dead serious, you'd come to believe I was crazy. After all, you know you can work, it's an obvious fact to you. If I involved other people, including relatives and doctors, you might start to feel persecuted and frightened. That is exactly the experience of many people with serious mental illness that I have interviewed. The neuropsychological deficits have left their concept of self, their beliefs about what they can and cannot do, literally stranded in time. They believe they have all the same abilities and the same prospects they enjoyed prior to the onset of the illness. That is why we hear such unrealistic plans for the future from our loved ones.

If a Man Can Mistake his Wife for a Hat...

If you have never talked to someone after they have suffered a stroke, brain tumor, or head injury, then what I have just said might seem difficult to believe. If so, I recommend that you read *The Man who Mistook his Wife for a Hat,* by the neurologist Oliver Sacks who is also the author of the book that was the basis for the movie, "Awakenings." Dr. Sacks has the gift of being able to describe in vivid detail the inner life of people who have suffered brain damage.

Writing about one case, which became the namesake for the book I recommended to you, he describes a man who had cancer in the visual parts of his brain. Dr. Sack's notes that when he first met Dr. P., a music professor, he couldn't think of why he was referred to his clinic for an evaluation. He appeared normal, there was nothing unusual about his speech and he displayed a high level of intelligence. However, as the neurological evaluation proceeded, bizarre perceptions emerged. When asked to put his shoes back on, he delayed, gazing at his foot with intense but misplaced concentration. When Dr. Sacks asked if he could help, Dr. P. declined his offer and continued looking around until he finally grabbed his foot and asked "This is my shoe, no?" When he was shown where his shoe was, he replied, "I thought that was my foot."

There was nothing wrong with Dr. P.'s vision, it was how his brain was constructing and categorizing his perceptions that was disturbed. Later, when he was sitting with his wife in Dr. Sack's office, he thought it was time to leave and reached for his hat. But instead of his hat, he grabbed his wife's head and tried to lift it off, to put it on. He had apparently mistaken his wife's head for a hat! When giving talks about poor insight in serious mental disorders I often like to say: If brain damage can cause a man to mistake his wife for a hat, it is easy to imagine how it can cause someone to mistake their *past-self* for their *current-self.*

In the late 1980's, I worked extensively with neurological patients administering psychological tests designed to uncover the deficits caused by brain damage. I couldn't help but notice the similarities between the neurological syndrome of *anosognosia* and poor insight in persons with serious mental illness. Anosognosia bears a striking resemblance to the type of poor insight we have been discussing. This resemblance includes both symptomatic and neurological similarities. For example, patients with anosognosia will frequently give strange explanations, or what neurologists call *confabulations*, to explain any observations that contradict their belief that they are not ill.

One forty-two-year-old man I evaluated had suffered a serious head injury that damaged tissue in the right frontal, parietal and temporal lobes of this brain. I met with him about one week after the car accident that had left him paralyzed on the left side of his body. When I asked him if he could raise his left arm for me he answered "yes." When I asked him to do it, he lay there expressionless unable to move his paralyzed arm. I pointed out that he had not moved his arm. He disagreed. So I asked him to do it again while looking at his arm. When he saw that he could not move his arm he said "You've tied it down."

When one's conception of who they are gets stranded in time, cut off from important new information, they can't help but ignore or explain away any evidence that contradicts their self-concept.

Anosognosia has been with us for as long our species has enjoyed the benefits of consciousness. More than 2,000 years ago, L.A. Seneca, writing on the moral implications of self-beliefs described what appears to be a case of anosognosia following hemianopia (blindness caused by brain damage): *"Incredible as it might appear...She does not know that she is blind. Therefore, again and again she asks her guardian to take her elsewhere. She claims that my home is dark."* How could someone not realize that they are blind? And why, when faced with the evidence, would they seek to explain away the blindness?

The man who had the car accident that left him paralyzed, could not understand that he could no longer move the left side of his body. It didn't fit with what he felt (that his arm and leg worked fine), so he couldn't help but try to explain away any evidence to the contrary. He is just like the blind woman who did not understand that she was blind, and more easily believed in alternative explanations (the house is kept dark) than the truth. Every day, someone with a serious mental illness utters similar explanations to buttress their belief that there is nothing wrong with them. When one's conception of who they are gets stranded in time, cut off from important new information, they can't help but ignore or explain away any evidence that contradicts their self-concept. And so many chronically mentally ill persons attribute their hospitalizations to fights with parents, misunderstandings, etc.. Like neurological patients with anosognosia, they appear rigid in their unawareness, unable to integrate new information contrary to their erroneous beliefs.

One final similarity between neurological patients with anosognosia and the seriously mentally ill involves the patch-like pattern of poor insight. Pockets of unawareness and awareness often coexist side by side, in both anosognosia patients, and in the seriously mentally ill. For example, the anosognosia patient may be aware of a memory deficit, but unaware of paralysis. Similarly, we have seen many patients with schizophrenia who are aware of particular symptoms while remaining completely unaware of others.

Damage to particular brain areas can result in anosognosia. Studies of anosognosia provide a practical starting point for hypothesizing about the brain structures responsible for insight in persons with serious mental disorders. Neurological patients with anosognosia are frequently found to have lesions (i.e. damage of one kind or another) to the frontal lobes of their brain. Interestingly, research has shown that these same areas of the brain are often dysfunctional in people with serious mental illness.

In a study of neurological patients at Hillside Hospital in New York City conducted in collaboration with Dr. William Barr and Dr. Alexandra Economou, I compared patterns of unawareness in three groups of patients suffering damage to three different regions of the brain. This study was funded by the Stanley Foundation and had as one of its goals identifying brain dysfunction most likely to produce awareness deficits. As expected, patients with frontal lesions were more likely to show problems with insight into their illness than patients with left posterior damage. Lets look at an example.

George, a seventy-one-year-old man who had suffered a stroke was asked to draw the clock on the left side of the figure that appears below. Before drawing the clock, he was asked "Do you think you will have any difficulty copying of this picture?"

George was instructed to use the following 4 point scale to answer the question: 0 = no difficulty, 1= some difficulty, 2 = much difficulty, and 3 cannot do. He answered "0," and said he would have no difficulty. The right side of figure one shows the drawing he made after exerting great effort.

More striking than his inability to recognize that the stroke had left him unable to perform such a simple task, is was happened next. When asked if he had any difficulty drawing the clock, he answered: "No, not at all." Further questioning revealed that he could not see, or comprehend, the differences between his clock and ours. When it was pointed out to him that his numbers drifted past the circle, he became slightly flustered and said "Wait, that can't be my drawing. What happened to the one I drew?"

In his book *The Principals of Psychology*, William James wrote: *Whilst part of what we perceive comes through our senses from the object before us, another part (and it may be the larger part) always comes from our own mind.* There are few better examples of James' insight than the one I have just given you. George "saw" his drawing using the sense of vision. But his perception of the clock, the image of the drawing that was processed in his brain, was something all together *He was operating under beliefs that were linked to his past-self rather than his current-self.* different than what his eyes saw. George had a concept of himself, a *self-schema,* that included the belief that he could easily copy a simple drawing of a clock. You have the same belief as part of your self-schema. You might not consider yourself artistically endowed, but you believe that you could reproduce a reasonable facsimile of the drawing if asked to. In a sense, this belief was stranded in George's brain, disconnected from his visual senses and left unmodified by the stroke that he had suffered. He was operating under beliefs that were linked to his *past-self* rather than his *current-self.* He *saw* the numbers drifting outside his lopsided circle, but he *perceived* the numbers to be in their proper place inside a symmetrical circle. Our brains are built to order, and even help construct our perceptions.

Here is a simple example of what I am talking about. Answer this question: What letter appears in the box you see here? If you answered "E" you saw what the majority of people who are given this task see. But in reality, you did not *see* the letter E. What you saw is a line with

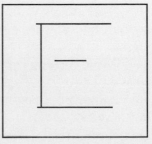

two right angles (a box-like version of the letter "C") and a short line that is unconnected to the longer one. Yet, you likely answered E because you *perceived* the letter E. The visual processing and memory circuits of your brain closed the gap between the lines so you could answer my question.

To prove that poor insight in serious mental disorders is neurologically based, we need more than observed similarities with neurological patients. We need testable hypotheses and data that are confirmatory. Knowing that patients with schizophrenia frequently show poor performance on neuropsychological tests of frontal lobe function, we hypothesized that there should be a strong correlation between various aspects of unawareness of illness and performance on these tests of frontal function. Dr Donald Young and his colleagues in Toronto Canada quickly tested and confirmed our hypothesis. They studied patients with schizophrenia to examine whether performance on neuropsychological tests of frontal lobe function predicted the level of insight into illness. The results indicated that poor performance on tests of frontal lobe function was associated with lower levels of insight. Of particular note is the fact that this correlation was independent of other cognitive functions tested including overall IQ. In other words, poor insight was related to dysfunction of the frontal lobes of the brain, rather than to a more generalized problem with intellectual functioning. Taken together, these results strongly support the idea that poor insight into illness and resulting treatment refusal stem from a mental defect rather than informed choice.

But just as one swallow does not make a summer, one research finding does not make an indisputable fact. The next step in determining more definitively whether poor insight into illness is a consequence of frontal lobe dysfunction is to test the hypothesis as Young and his colleagues have done. It requires that the finding is replicated in a new group of patients. As it turns out, as of this writing, the finding that poorer insight is highly correlated with frontal lobe dysfunction has been replicated more than ten times by different research groups. Repeated replications by independent researchers are infrequent in psychiatric research. The fact that different researchers have found essentially the same thing as Young and his colleagues, speaks to the strength of the relationship between insight and the frontal lobes of the brain.

Only two studies have not found this relationship, but methodological flaws in the design of the research are likely the reason. The research discussed above, and other newer studies that link poor insight to structural brain abnormalities, lead us to only one conclusion. In most patients with schizophrenia and related psychotic disorders, deficits in insight and resulting non-adherence to treatment, stem from a broken brain, rather than stubbornness or denial.

A Broken Brain Is Easier to "Fix"

The bottom line to all of this research is that more likely than not, a broken brain is creating barriers to insight and acceptance of treatment in the mentally ill person you're trying to help. There are two immediate ways in which you can use this knowledge to benefit your loved one and yourself. First, when faced with the frustration of trying to convince her to get help, remember *the enemy is brain dysfunction*, not the person. This shift in your thinking can go a long way toward lowering your level of frustration, increasing your effectiveness, and building a collaborative relationship with the person you are trying to help. Secondly, this knowledge can be used to rekindle your hope in your ability to help your loved one accept the help being offered. Hope? If you're like most people, the research I reviewed above may have left you feeling more pessimistic or confused than optimistic! Brain damage is irreparable, isn't it ? If poor insight in this context is another symptom of brain dysfunction, then what is there to hope for?

A common myth is that personality stubbornness or defensiveness, are far easier to fix then deficits caused by brain damage. In fact, it is far more difficult to change a person's personality than to teach them ways to compensate for some forms of brain dysfunction. So, although the notion

In fact, it is far more diffi-cult to change a person's personality than to teach them ways to compensate for some forms of brain dys-function.

that brain dysfunction can cause poor insight may at first lead you to feel power-less, it is actually grounds for renewed hope. Rehabilitation is possible following many types of brain damage. Not because brain cells are repaired, but because func-tions can be re-routed to other parts of the brain that are undamaged. In such cases, a careful assessment of the deficits caused by the lesions is made, and a plan to com-pensate for the loss of ability is devised. This is usual prac-tice following strokes, brain tumors, head injuries, and other causes of central nervous system damage. In fact, rehabilita-tion specialists are trained specifically for this task, which is frequently referred to as *cognitive remediation*.

One such patient I worked with had suffered a head injury following a bicycle accident. David, a twenty-four-year-old messenger, would have escaped his collision with a taxicab in New York City completely unscathed if he had been wearing a helmet. However, he had not been wearing a helmet, and the resulting brain damage left him with moder-ate impairments in short-term memory. For example, he could not remember where he parked his car once it was out of his sight, or why he had gone to the grocery store or bank by the time he got there. Remembering the names of people he had just met, appointments, and other bits of new infor-mation we all need to remember to function day-to-day, was seemingly impossible for David. His long-term memory was fine, however. He remembered the birthdays of close friends and relatives, details of places and events from his past, and other information that had been stored before the accident. As you might imagine, recording new information into long-term memory was now much more difficult for him because he often could not hold the new information in his short-term memory long enough to encode it, or file it away. One might worry that David was doomed to live the rest of his life befuddled and confused, like an absent minded professor who would forget his head if it weren't connected to his neck. But, like the absent minded professor, David had other cognitive skills and character traits that could be recruited to help with his memory problems.

First, and foremost, he was motivated for rehabilitation. He was frustrated that he could not remember things, and wanted to get better at it. Second, he could focus his attention and concentrate for short periods of time without any problem. His short term visual memory was relatively less impaired than verbal memory. So, although he could not remember a list of words he had read ten minutes earlier, he could easily recall pictures and shapes. Also, once something got into long-term memory, it usually stayed there. With a rough understanding of his abilities and disabilities, a plan was devised to help David to improve his memory. He learned to use memory aids, or mnemonics, to improve his short term memory.

Since he could focus and had the ability to remember visual information, he was taught to visualize the information (words) he wanted to remember. Remembering where he parked his car was easy when he used this strategy. Rather than trying to remember row letters and parking space numbers, he would create a map of the parking lot in his head and visualize where his car was in the square or rectangle he saw in his mind's eye. By visualizing the lot from above, he could locate his car with ease. I helped him to develop the habit of carrying a notepad in his pocket and writing down anything he needed to remember. To counter the problem of David forgetting to look at his reminder list, we set his watch alarm to beep every 30 minutes. Whenever he heard the beep he remembered, after a little practice, to look at his reminder list. David also learned to visualize names and words to help him remember. Having just met someone named Tom, he visualized a tom-tom drum. Carol was transformed into a group of Christmas carolers, a friend's newborn infant named Elizabeth became the Queen of England, John a toilet, Jack a car-jack, etc.. To remember to meet a friend at a

McDonald's at five o'clock, he pictured five golden arches. He got so good at visualizing that he would often make a game of it, challenging others to see if they could come up with an image to match a name or phrase.

This approach is highly relevant to the task of helping the seriously mentally ill develop awareness of the illness, and the new skills they will need to become willing and active participants in their own treatment. In the chapters that come next, you will learn how to evaluate the nature and severity of the awareness deficits your loved one has, and to devise a plan for helping her to compensate for these deficits. With this method, you can help her develop the kind of insight that she needs to cope effectively with the illness. Accomplishing this can be much easier than you might think.

Part II
How to Help them to
Accept Treatment

Chapter 5
A New Approach

D r. Karen Holloway sighed and said "Michael's back" as she walked toward where I was sitting in the nurse's station. "I need you to go to the E.R. and do his admission," she added.

"Michael Kass?" I asked, incredulous.

"Afraid so," Karen replied, a bit bemused by my surprise. "Get used to it, Xavier, some patients are stuck in the revolving door, and Michael's one of them."

Karen was the Chief Resident at the hospital in New York City where I was an intern in 1988. She is one of the more compassionate, bright, and level-headed clinicians with whom I have ever had the pleasure of working. The diagnosis of "Revolving Door Patient" was not one that she made lightly or without compassion. Michael Kass had been discharged from the hospital only six weeks earlier after a one-month hospitalization. When he left, he was no longer hearing voices. His delusions still lingered, but he felt little pressure to talk about them, and he was set to receive follow-up treatment in one of our outpatient clinics. Judging by Karen's comment, I guess I didn't hide my disappointment and surprise that he was back so soon.

I took the stairs two at a time, eight floors down, to the Emergency Room, no use waiting for the overburdened elevators, and walked to the far corner to the door labeled "Psych. E.R." Behind this door was a suite of five rooms that were sequestered from the rest of the service, with four patient bays to the left and the nurses' station to the right. As I entered I quickly took a right and ducked into the nurses station. I didn't want Michael to know I was there until I had a chance to talk to the triage nurse. The report I got was frustrating to hear.

After leaving the hospital, Michael went home to live with his parents, but he never showed up for his follow-up appointment. His parents, in their late sixties, didn't know that Michael hadn't gone to see his doctor. They asked about his appointment, but he never wanted to talk about it. They called the clinic, but no one would speak to them about whether or not their thirty-five-year-old son had gone to his doctor's appointment. They also didn't know that after the one-week supply of medications he had been given from the hospital ran out, he never had the prescription refilled.

I spent about twenty minutes looking at his old chart, which the triage nurse had ordered up from medical records. Then I stepped out of the nurses' station and greeted my new-old patient.

"Hi Michael, how are you?"

"Dr. Amadorafloor! What are you doing here?" he answered, *clanging*[7], laughing, and talking a mile a minute. "You've got to get me out of here! I was minding my own business - I wasn't hurting anyone - the police got it all wrong. Get me out of here OK? You've got to get me out because..."

"Michael, Michael, hold on, wait up a minute!" I tried to interrupt.

"...I'm not supposed to be *beer*. They'll find me here if I stay. Gotta go, gotta get out, OK?"

"Michael, try to slow down and tell me what happened. OK?"

"I'm telling you what happened. I'm not supposed to be here." he shot back annoyed with me.

It took almost an hour to get through the checklist I was trained to use. I completed a *mental status exam*[8], evaluat-

---

7. A feature of thought disorder, a frequent symptom of psychosis, that involves word associations based on rhyme.
8. A cornerstone of psychiatric assessment, the mental status exam involves an assessment of the clarity of consciousness, memory, attention, emotion, thought process, insight into illness, and various symptoms of mental illness.

ed his current symptoms, and listened to his version of what had happened and why he was in the Psych. E.R.. Excusing myself while he was pleading with me to get him out again, I escaped to the nurses' station to write down what I had learned.

Michael was once again hearing voices of government agents who were commenting on his every move. While we were talking, I asked him what the voices were saying, and he repeated, "he is sitting on the bed, talking with that doctor, he can't escape us now." Given the voices he was hearing it is not surprising that he developed the delusion that some secret Federal agency was monitoring his movements and planning to assassinate him.

I noted in his chart the re-emergence of the hallucinations and exacerbation of the longstanding delusion about government agents persecuting him. I also noted that he was not currently suicidal or homicidal, his insight into illness was poor, and a number of other observations I had made while interviewing him. My written recommendation was to restart the antipsychotic medication he had been on when he was discharged six weeks ago, and to admit him to our in-patient psychiatric unit "for stabilization." I went back to see Michael, told him my recommendation, and asked him to sign himself into the hospital for a couple of weeks. He refused.

"The only thing wrong with me is that I'm going to get killed if I stay here any longer!"

Since he had been found hiding in a subway train tunnel and had struggled with police when they extracted him, I thought we had a fairly good case for an involuntary admission. When he was found, he hadn't eaten or bathed in several days and he had made camp dangerously close to an active track explaining to police that "they [Federal agents] would never think to look for me here." I called Dr. Holloway; she agreed, and the appropriate papers were signed to admit him against his will for 72 hours. If he didn't want to stay after the 72 hours, and if at that time we felt he was still a danger to himself because of his mental illness, we would take him before a mental health court and try to get a judge to order thirty days of involuntary treatment.

When the plan was explained to Michael, he understandably went ballistic. He was terribly frightened and felt certain that he would be killed if he stayed in the hospital. However, after accepting medication by injection, he calmed down considerably; and was moved upstairs to the psychiatric ward.

Michael's story is fairly typical. I was operating under a medical model that focused on the tasks of diagnosis and treatment. Once the diagnosis and treatment to be offered are decided upon, the patient is informed of both. If the patient refuses, and fits the legal criteria for an involuntary admission to a hospital, the doctors take charge. In some cases, medical doctors operating under a benevolent paternal ethic are able to order treatment against a person's wishes. Like a parent who knows best for her child, the physician can take control by admitting the person and treating them against their will. This is a more dramatic instance of similar laws we abide by everyday (e.g., laws that require seatbelts, mandatory rabies inoculation of pets, motorcycle helmets, prohibit drunk driving, etc.).

My next task under this model was to educate Michael about his illness and the need for treatment. If you are reading this book, then you know that when it comes to individuals like Michael, education about the illness does not translate into insight into one's own illness. And, indeed, that is what happened over the two-week period that Michael was in the hospital.

I told him all about delusions and hallucinations and confronted him about his "denial" of the illness. I explained to him the nature of the problems he had and why he should accept the treatment being offered. Like the previous hospitalization, once he became more stable, he readily agreed that he would take the medication when he left the hospital. When I would confront him and say, "I think you're just saying that so you can get out of here," he would sometimes sheepishly admit to the lie and tell me that there was nothing

wrong with him except the
fact that people wouldn't
leave him alone. But most
often he would stick to the
party line and say, "I know
the medication helps me and
that I need to take it."
Ironically, as some of his
symptoms responded to the
medication, he got better at
consistently feigning alle-
giance to the doctor's orders.

> *For people with serious
> mental illness who are
> unaware of the illness, this
> traditional approach rarely
> works. It rests on the mis-
> taken assumption that the
> patient has come to see the
> doctor because he feels he has
> a problem and wants help.*

For people with serious mental illness who are unaware
of the illness, this traditional approach rarely works. It rests
on the mistaken assumption that the patient has come to see
the doctor because he feels he has a problem and wants help.
It assumes a collaborative approach from the start: the doctor as an ally, not an adversary.

Collaboration is a Goal Not a Given

In my experience, it is often easy to change such adversarial relationships into an alliance. It takes some focused
effort, but it's not hard to do. The first step is to build a collaborative relationship with the ultimate goal of arriving at
an agreed-upon "plan of action." Ideally, this is a mutual,
and realistic, understanding of the treatment that will be
accepted: i.e., a treatment-agreement. But before a treatment-agreement can be forged, a plan of action that does not
necessarily involve taking medication may have to come
first.

The four-step process you will learn about involves listening, empathizing, finding areas where the two of you
agree, and ultimately forming a partnership to achieve the
goals you share. I developed this four-step strategy based on
the scientific evidence I discussed in the last chapter and
from nearly twenty years of personal and clinical experience. So that you have an overview of what you can do and
how it will work, I give a brief description of each step here.

L.E.A.P. Four Steps to Creating a Treatment Agreement

1. Listen
2. Empathize
3. Agree
4. Partnership

Listen

Effective listening is really a skill that needs to be cultivated. You will need to learn to really listen to what your loved one feels, wants, and believes in. Listening without learning is pointless. First, you need to walk in the other person's shoes to gain a clear idea of *their* experience of the illness and treatment. For the uninitiated, this is not as easy as it may sound on the face of it. Too many times we make assumptions without checking them out with the person about whom we are making assumptions. Knowledge is power. When you know how someone experiences the idea of having a mental illness and taking psychiatric drugs, you will have obtained the leverage you need to begin to build a treatment agreement.

> *The first step involves walking in the other person's shoes to gain a clear idea of their experience of the illness and treatment.*

But you will also need to know what their hopes and expectations are for the future, whether or not you believe they're realistic. And finally, you want to identify the cognitive deficits (e.g., problems with memory, attention, focusing thoughts) that are creating barriers between you and the person you're concerned about and between that person and effective treatment.

Empathize

The second step involves learning when and how to express empathy. If there were a moral to each step and chapter, this one would go something like this: If you want someone to seriously consider your point of view, be certain he feels you have seriously considered his. Quid pro quo. That means that you must empathize with all of the reasons he has for not wanting to accept treatment,

If you want someone to seriously consider your point of view, be certain he feels you have seriously considered his. Quid pro quo.

even the "crazy" ones. But don't worry; empathizing with how a particular delusion makes one feel is not the same as agreeing that the belief is true. This may seem like a minor point, but, as you will learn, the right kind of empathy will make a tremendous difference on how receptive your loved one is to your concerns and opinions. In the chapter devoted to this step, I give you step-by-step instructions on how to do this using techniques such as *reflective listening*.

Agree

Find common ground and stake it out. Knowing that what *you want* for the other person is something *she does not want* for herself can make it seem as if there is no common ground. She doesn't think she needs medication or therapy, and you think she does. Like any conflict of beliefs between two people, to resolve the disagreement to your satisfaction requires that

Your focus is on making observations together, identifying facts that you can ultimately agree upon.

you discover what motivation the other person has to change. Common ground always exists even between the most extreme opposing positions.

The emphasis is on acknowledging that your loved one has personal choice and responsibility for the decisions he makes about his life. During this step, you become a neutral observer, pointing out the various positive and negative consequences of decisions your loved one has made. That means refraining from saying things like, "see if you had taken your medication, you wouldn't have ended up in the hospital." Your focus is on *making observations together* - identifying facts upon which you can ultimately agree. Rather than making an observation or statement about what happened you ask a lot of questions such as "So what happened after you decided to stop taking your medication?" "Did the voices quiet down after you stopped?" "How long after stopping the medication was it before you went to the hospital?" If you are truly collaborating, asking questions rather than giving advice or direction comes a lot easier than it may sound.

Partnership

Forming a partnership for recovery is the last and, in my experience, the most satisfying step in this process. The aim of this step is to help you to collaborate on accomplishing the goals you agreed

The aim of this step is to help you to collaborate on accomplishing the goals you agreed upon.

upon. Unlike the previous steps, this one involves both you and your loved one making an explicit decision to work together and to become teammates against a common opponent. You may call the enemy different names, but the names are irrelevant to arriving at a plan of action. The final step culminates in arriving at a treatment agreement.

Chapter 6

Listen

I t was 7:30 am and morning rounds had begun on the ward where I worked as an attending psychologist. The entire day shift was seated in a circle around the room. Doctors, nurses, social workers, and assorted students were currently, or soon would be, repeating this ritual on in-patient psychiatric wards all over the country.

The chief of the unit, a psychiatrist, called the meeting to order and then Marie, the head nurse, took over. She began by reviewing how each patient had fared the night before. When she came to Samantha, a forty-year-old, single woman with chronic schizophrenia, she paused and sighed before beginning "Samantha Green, stable on 6 milligrams of Risperidol, she slept well last night and is ready for discharge today. Jo Anna, do you want to fill everyone in on the discharge plan?" she asked the senior social worker.

"Sure. It's a real gem." she answered sarcastically. "Samantha is going back to her parents house and has an out-patient appointment with her doctor set for a week from today. Mr. and Mrs. Greene are picking her up at noon and she's walking out the door with a one week supply of med-ication."

"You don't sound too pleased with the plan," I started to say.

"It's nothing personal," she interrupted knowing that Samantha and her parents also had an appointment with me for a family meeting. "The plan is alright, it's Samantha I'm not pleased with!" she paused, and then added, "Look we all know what's going to happen. Call me cynical but I'll bet you ten dollars she stops taking her medication before the end of the month and she'll be back here before you know it.

She needs long-term hospitalization, not another trip through the revolving door."

Samantha had been admitted to the hospital four times in the past year. Each of the episodes of illness was triggered when she secretly stopped taking her medication. Her parents would notice her talking to herself and start to worry that she was not taking her pills. Her mother would then ask if this was so, and Samantha always denied it even though she had not taken them for weeks. By the time the truth came out, it was usually too late and hospitalization was needed.

To my ears, Jo Anna's lack of faith in Samantha, her parents, and in me was neither cynical nor insulting. Given Jo Anna's experience and perspective she would have been foolish to expect anything more than she did. However, if Jo Anna knew what I knew, she might have shared my optimism for Samantha and her family.

I knew the reasons Samantha didn't want to take psychiatric drugs. It took some effort to uncover the true reasons, but with that knowledge and a good idea of what Samantha wanted out of life, I knew I could help her to stay on her medication, in treatment, and out of the hospital. But Jo Anna and the rest of the hospital staff hadn't learned what I had because they were focusing on other things.

In the climate of managed care and increasing advances in drug therapies for serious mental illness, mental health professionals working in hospitals have become increasingly specialized. Psychiatrists evaluate health and symptoms and order medications.[9]

Psychologists working on in-patient wards typically perform psychological assessments and less often do therapy. Nurses dispense medications, monitor patients' health and safety and provide education about the treatments

---

9.   In my experience, this is not all that psychiatrists do. But more and more the trend in American psychiatry is to focus on pharmacotherapy rather than psychotherapy, especially when treating the seriously mentally ill. Unfortunately, a discussion of why this has happened and the advantages and disadvantages reaped is beyond the scope of this book.

received. Social workers evaluate the patient's discharge needs and make arrangements for out-patient treatment and residence. As a psychologist working with the seriously mentally ill, I know a good deal about medications used to treat the disorder but I can't prescribe them. My job is different. Understanding the person and how the illness has affected his cognitive capacities and sense of self is my area of focus. And that is why I was optimistic about stopping the revolving door Samantha was stuck inside.

Unlike the others, I knew how Samantha experienced being ill and what she thought about the drugs we were "pushing" on her. I also had a clear understanding of what it was she wanted out of life. In other words, I had been doing a lot of listening and what I had learned gave me a foothold with Samantha and good reason to have hope.

STEP 1. Listen

The cornerstone of building a treatment agreement that will work and outlast your direct involvement is cut from the quarry of your loved one's sense of who she is, and what she is capable of doing. Unless you know its shape, color, texture and strength, you will be unable to build on this foundation. Each stone you lay will topple and fall to the ground unless you have listened and learned about her:

- beliefs about having a mental illness
- attitudes about medication
- concept of what she can and cannot do
- hopes and expectations for the future
- cognitive deficits caused by the illness

As you will learn in the next few chapters, knowledge of these five areas can be put to practical use. Depending on what you learn, different techniques are suggested. A cautionary note however, don't try to get this information without first reading about how you might want to go about doing it. Because serious mental illness interferes with a person's ability to communicate effectively, there are some opportunities and pitfalls you want to watch out for.

How to Listen and Learn

We all know how to listen. But what I describe here is very different than the usual kind of listening we engage in from day to day. The main difference is that it is listening for the sole purpose of understanding what the other person is trying to convey. It is an active, rather than passive, process. I'll explain.

For whatever reasons, I am a naturally good listener. All my life people have told me this. As a psychotherapist, I pride myself in my ability to listen and to understand other people's experience. You may also believe, for good reason, that you are also a good listener, but everything I thought I knew about listening was put to the test the first few times I tried to converse with people suffering from serious mental illness.

I was twenty-three years-old when I took a job as a "psychiatric technician" (a.k.a. nursing aid) on an in-patient psychiatric ward at the University of Arizona Health Sciences Center. My brother's first psychotic episode was less than a year prior and despite his rambling speech and crazy ideas, I could still understand him. Or so I thought at the time. Despite my youthful confidence, my inadequacies as a listener were brought home during my first week at work.

Usually when listening to other people we don't have to deal with the issues and emotions that are common when conversing with someone with schizophrenia, depression, or mania. As a therapy aid I was responsible of assessing, among other things, how agitated, depressed, elated, suicidal, or dangerous my patients were. I was also charged with the task of assessing whether the patients I worked with were following the prescribed treatment plan. Every conversation had a hidden agenda. I was so busy trying to get the information that I was supposed to get that I missed a lot of very important things.

My very first admission evaluation was with a forty-two-year-old woman who was in the throws of a grandiose delusion and an irritable manic episode. She was talking a mile a minute about her power to read minds, her supernatural abilities, and the fact that she didn't want to be in the hospital. She was very angry about being in the hospital. With a bright-red, hospital-issued clipboard on my knee, I diligently started with the list of questions that were printed neatly in rows.

"Can you tell me why you came to the hospital?"

"Can you tell me why you came to the hospital?" she mimicked with disdain, effectively making me feel humiliated for being a rookie.

"I am sorry. You were brought here by the police. That's right isn't it?" I quickly countered trying to recover my composure.

"I am sorry. You were brought here by the police. That's right isn't it?" she echoed sarcastically.

"It sounds like you don't want to talk right now. I am sorry, but I have to get through these questions." I pleaded with her despite the fact that I was feeling even more humiliated and more than a touch angry.

"I don't give a shit about your fucking questions!" she spat at me. "I am sorry but I really do need to get through these questions," she mimicked sarcastically. "Grow up little boy. You better realize who you're dealing with here. You don't know what you've gotten yourself into and you are in way over your head. Way over your head. Maybe I'll have your head. I could you know. It's as easy as snapping my fingers or blinking an eye or squashing the wings of a butterfly!" she shouted rapid fire then burst out hysterically laughing.

My agenda was moot and my face was a bright shade of red. I know because she made a point of telling me as I was excusing myself and trying to walk, not run, out the door. I was scared, embarrassed that my co-workers could hear her yelling, and angry. I went to the nurses station and plopped down next to Nancy, the charge nurse.

"You got that done fast." she said incredulously.

"Not really. I didn't get much done at all."

"She wouldn't answer your questions?"

"No. All she did was mimic my every word and threaten me."

"Threaten you!"

"Not exactly. At least not in reality. She was threatening me with her God-like delusional powers." I quickly corrected Nancy's misperception.

"Well, it seems like she may not be able to answer these questions right now. What did you learn about her from just sitting in the room?"

"Well, she's angry and doesn't want to be here. She's manic, irritable and grandiose. And she doesn't want to talk to me. Maybe someone else should give it a shot?"

"No. She's your patient. I just gave her some   Haldol. Give her a couple of hours to calm down a little, then try again. Only this time, don't bring in the admission form. Start by asking her if there is anything she would like to say. Let her talk for a while and see where it goes. Look for an opening - a moment where she is asking you a question. Try to engage her."

I took Nancy's advice and ultimately learned quite a bit about Barbara. That was her name, Barbara. It took making the time to listen and putting my agenda on the back burner so I could listen to what she was feeling about being forced to be a patient in a psychiatric hospital when she had "better things to do." I also was able to get my form filled out. Some questions were not answered, but the essentials were covered.

It's hard to listen in the face of all the distracting noise of psychosis, especially if you are pursuing an agenda and trying to follow a timetable. But it's not impossible. Listening is a skill and like any skill, practice makes perfect. The following listening guidelines will help you to deal with the unique problems that come when you try to understand and listen to someone with serious mental illness.

Listening Guidelines

1. Set Aside the Time
2. Agree on an Agenda
3. Listen for Beliefs about the Self and the Illness
4. Don't React
5. Let Chaos Be
6. Echo What You've Heard
7. Write it Down.

Set aside the time. Make appointments to discuss specific issues (e.g., "I'd like to talk with you after dinner about how you're feeling about your doctor. I'm curious about how it's going. That okay with you?") and times to simply "hang out" together (e.g., "Want to take a walk with me?") Specific appointments to talk, when possible, are best. If you're a therapist it is easier, you set an appointment. If you're a family member you might try having a cup of coffee or tea, a smoke, a walk, or do just about anything together to create a low-stress opportunity to talk.

Sometimes, especially when the illness flare-up, a "sit-down" conversation is impossible. In those instances, you can ask to sit nearby to read the newspaper. What you convey is that you can be together, perhaps even share a few words together, without any pressure or agenda. If you insist on having an agenda then let your agenda be to not have an agenda! This kind of interaction, though seemingly fruitless, builds trust and openness.

Agree on an agenda. If you can't agree on an agenda, then focus on listening. This builds rapport and trust, making it more likely that common ground can be found. When your loved one trusts that you will not pontificate about what he should and should not be doing he will

> *If you insist on having an agenda then let your agenda be to not have an agenda! This kind of interaction, though seemingly fruitless, builds trust and openness.*

be more apt to agree to talk about certain "hot" topics (e.g., his refusal of medicine). Agreeing on an agenda is easy if you follow your loved one's lead. For example, if he is upset about having to take medicine ask to talk with him about his feelings, not about the medicine or your belief that he should take it. You can say "I'd like to understand why you hate taking your medicine. Would you mind talking with me about it? I promise I won't pressure you or bug you - I really just want to understand how you feel about it." If he agrees, then you have set up an agenda together (to talk about why he dislikes taking medicine).

Listen for beliefs about the self and the illness. Understanding how your loved one sees herself, and her beliefs about whether or not she is ill, is the key to unlocking her isolation and to building an alliance. It's very easy once you know what to look for. You want to learn about what she thinks about taking psychiatric medications. Does it make her feel weak or like a failure? Is she embarrassed by them? Does she like anything about the medication? Does it help her to feel less frightened or help with sleep? How does she feel about herself when she takes the pills? Does she think she needs to take medication and if so for how long? Are there some troubling side effects to the medication that are really bothering her that she might not have mentioned yet?

It is also vital that you find out what she wants out of life without being judgmental. What does she aspire to? You need to find out what it is that is most important to her. If she tells you she wants to work, don't jump in and say, like I once did with my brother Henry, "That's not realistic! You haven't had a job in ten years!" Just listen and learn.

Don't react. I don't mean you should ignore what you're hearing, just don't jump in with your opinion like I did with my brother. Try not to react. When I give lectures to families and therapists, this bit of advice often confuses people and makes them frustrated with me.

During one such lecture to a group of psychiatric residents, I made the point that in order to learn about someone's delusions, and their experience of being in hospital and on medications, you sometimes had to let them have the mistaken impression that you believe in their delusions. This proposition was met with disbelief and outrage by one young doctor who interrupted me and asked, "Are you saying we should agree with our patients' delusions? That's not ethical!"

"No, I didn't say agree. Just don't disagree." I clarified.

"Okay. I have a new patient who believes that the voices he hears are that of Satan. He believes that he has been chosen by God to save us all from the devil who is taking possession of people's minds and souls one by one. He told me this morning that all of the other patients on the ward and three of the nurses are already possessed and that he must fast for thirty days to drive the devil out of them."

I interrupted his story and asked, "What did you say to him?"

"I told him that I didn't think the devil had taken over anyone. I reassured him that he was safe and told him that he had to eat."

"Why did you feel the need to say those things?"

"Because what he believed wasn't true and he was planning to starve himself!"

"So what if his beliefs were not true? Why the need to argue the point right now?"

"First of all I was trying to give him some reality testing. You know... help him to live in the same world as the rest of us. Secondly, I didn't want him to starve himself."

"But you haven't really answered my question. What was the urgency? You said he was a new patient so presumably you've started giving him antipsychotic medication."

"Yes." he answered.

"So why try to talk him out of the delusion. Why not give the medication time to work and focus instead on understanding his experience? And if your answer is that he was going to starve himself you know that you wouldn't have let that happen while he was under your care and in the hospital."

"I see your point about my jumping the gun. But what if I didn't say those things, what if I didn't tell him that I didn't share his beliefs? He might think that I believed the same thing."

"So what?."

"But that would be unethical. I can't collude with his delusions."

"I am not suggesting you tell him you also believe the patients and several nurses are possessed by the devil, just don't make a point of disagreeing with the belief. Of course he may back you into a corner by asking you if you think he sounds crazy. But even then you can say that anything is possible and for right now you only want to understand what he's thinking and how he's feeling. You agree that anything is possible don't you?"

"Sure. But everything isn't plausible or likely."

"Exactly. Do I think all your patients and a few of the nurses on your ward are possessed? Of course not because it's highly implausible and improbable. But anything is possible and that gives us the latitude we need to listen to our patients without judging, correcting, or otherwise interrupting the flow of information we are trying to listen to."

My brother once told me that my mother was the devil and her eyes were laser beams that could slice a person in half if you looked into them. I can't tell you how hard it was for me to not try and straighten him out. But I didn't have time to try and talk him out of this delusion. I was too busy trying to understand why he had stopped taking his medication and looking for a way to convince him to go back on them. All I could do was reassure him that he was safe and listen closely for a way in.

Let chaos be. Sometimes mental illness creates "thought disorder" making it difficult for others to follow the person's train of thought. When talking with someone who has thought disorder, or disorganized speech, be careful that you don't impose order on the chaos. Whenever someone says something that doesn't make sense to us, our natural tendency is to fill in the blanks or ask for clarification. In many cases involving people with serious mental illness, this normal reaction to chaotic discourse can mislead the listener and frustrate the speaker. If you feel like it is taking a lot of effort to understand what is being said, then you are trying too hard. It will take longer, but you will still get the information you need if you let the person with disorganized speech "ramble on." The trick is not to make too many inferences about the meaning of what is being said and to refrain from interrupting and guiding the conversation.

Echo what you've heard. When you make a point of communicating your understanding of what you have just heard, you insure that you have understood correctly and convey empathy. When its your turn to talk, simply repeat back what was said in your own words. If your loved one feels you understand her thoughts and feelings on a specific matter, she will be more open to hearing your opinion later.

Write it down. Writing down what you have learned will help you to separate the wheat from the chaff. I've made it very easy for you to do. Use the Attitudes and Beliefs Checklist (ABC) provided in the appendix to help you organize the information you get. It is often preferable to complete it *after* your conversations, but sometimes it is possible to do it during your talks if you believe your loved one won't get defensive. You can say, "I wanted to ask you some questions from this book I'm reading," and ask if it would be alright to take some notes. However, if you take this approach be prepared to reveal the title of this book and for any reaction you might get. The suggested questions given in the ABC are by no means the only way to get at the information you will need, but are provided as a rough guide. I strongly urge you to not skip this part of Step 1. Record what you are learning about your loved one's inner-life and his experience of the illness and treatment as it will help you to focus your efforts.

To illustrate, I offer the following two examples from families I have worked with. The first is a good example of how NOT to listen while the second provides an excellent lesson on how to do it right. Both examples are drawn from my work supervising therapists in training. Because my students typically bring video tapes of their sessions with families to our supervision meetings I can comment on both the therapist and the family members' listening skills.

Ineffective Listening

It was 3 o'clock and Dr. Brian Greene, a second-year resident in psychiatry, was meeting with Matt Blackburn and his parents. Matt is the twenty-six-year-old man who lives at home with his parents that I first told you about in Chapter 1. As you may recall, he was admitted to the hospital believing he was a close confidant of the U.S. President. He also believed that God had chosen him as his special messenger to world leaders, that the CIA was trying to assassinate him, and certain that his mother was trying to sabotage his mission (this belief was not entirely delusional). Also, his speech was disorganized and he was hearing voices when he was admitted to the hospital. Now, although the delusions were still present, his speech was more cogent and the voices had quieted down a bit. The meeting was called by Dr. Greene to discuss what Matt would do after being discharged from the hospital.

"Mr. Blackburn, Mrs. Blackburn," Brian said to each as he shook their hands. "Please come in and have a seat." Matt was already seated at the end of a long table in the patient dining room. His mother circled the table to reach her son and bent down to give him a kiss. Mr. Blackburn immediately sat down in the chair closest to him, at the other end of the table, and started asking questions of Dr. Greene.

"I know we're supposed to be talking about Matt's discharge but don't you think he needs to stay here longer? I don't think he's ready to come home yet."

"There's really nothing more we can offer him here, Mr. Blackburn." Brian answered.

"Well, I don't think he's ready and neither does his mother!"

"Hold on," Mrs. Blackburn said, "I didn't say that exactly. Of course we want you to come home," she added directing her last comment to Matt. "We're just worried about what's going to happen next."

Seizing the opportunity Brian began, "Matt has an appointment later this week with Dr. Remmers in our out-patient clinic, he has enough medicine with him to last until that appointment, and the hospital Day Program has accepted him. He can start there as soon as Dr. Remmers has seen him."

"This is exactly what I was afraid of." Matt's father said to his wife. He turned to face Brian and added, "I don't want to be negative Dr. Greene, but he'll never go to that appointment and he won't go to this day program your talking about. We need a better plan than this. Matt won't take his pills and he doesn't like hanging around the people in these programs. He says they're all crazy!"

"Matt. What do you have to say about all this?" Brian rightly asked.

"I said I'd go. I'll go!" he responded loudly while looking down at the table.

"That's what you promised us before Matt." his father said more kindly. "But when we get home you disappear into your room and you don't go anywhere."

"It's different this time. I'll go."

"Are you sure?" his mother asked looking worried.

"Yeah Mom, don't worry, I'll go. I really will. Okay?" Matt's father didn't look convinced, but his mother and doctor looked, if not convinced, at least placated by what they had just heard.

Lets review the seven listening guidelines I gave above. Did Dr. Greene and Matt's parents:

1. Set Aside the Time?

Brian and Matt's family did set aside a special time to talk. That was a plus. Sometimes people get discharged from the hospital and no such meetings take place. Another plus was that the meeting began in a collaborative way. Matt had been brought to the dining room by Brian and while the two of them waited for his parents Brian listened to Matt's concerns about the meeting. But when Mr. And Mrs. Blackburn entered the room, Brian shifted from a receptive dialogue (he was listening to Matt's worries) to a pro-active one (he set the agenda without Matt's help).

2. Agree on an Agenda?

Although it may have appeared that there was an agreed upon agenda, there wasn't. Brian wanted to communicate the details of the post-hospital treatment plans and "seal the deal" so to speak. Matt wanted to leave the hospital and was willing, if that's what it took, to take medicine for a time. How long he was willing to stay on the medicine was never determined because Matt did not trust his doctor and parents enough to be forthcoming and reveal what his true feelings were. Mr. Blackburn openly predicted that his son would stay on the medicine for less than one week while Brian guessed, or hoped, that Matt would be willing to follow doctor's orders for months to come.

Mr. Blackburn was pursuing an agenda of trying to convince Brian to hold Matt in the hospital longer. And although Mrs. Blackburn was focused on the same agenda, she was preoccupied with her guilt and was focused on not hurting or angering Matt. And what was Matt's agenda? No one asked so we really don't know, though I found out later.

3. Listen for Beliefs about the Self and the Illness?

Although Matt said he would go to his appointment and stay on the medication prescribed for him, no one asked him *why* he would do it, how he felt about it, or whether he thought it would do him good or harm. He was also not asked about why this time felt different for him. Was he just trying to get everybody off his back, as his father thought, or was this truly a change of heart? If the trio had asked Matt about why he felt different this time around the truth of the matter would have been revealed.

We might predict that, because of his low level of trust, Matt would not be entirely truthful in his responses to these questions even if they were asked. But if they had been asked and his responses were listened to carefully, the truth might have been revealed. More importantly, Matt would have felt listened to and that his opinion mattered. Regardless of his answers, such questions could have been followed up with statements that empowered Matt and acknowledged that he actually was the person in charge of his own fate (unless of course he became so ill that he was involuntarily committed to treatment). He may have felt that his position was understood and consequently a little more open to hearing advice.

After reviewing the videotape of their meeting, I met with Matt and told him: "Well you know it's your choice. You know what I think and I can't force you to do something you don't believe in. I wouldn't want to do that even if I could. I respect your right to make this decision for yourself. I know you told Dr. Greene and your parents that you would stay on the medicine. But if you change your mind, and if I had to guess I'd guess that you probably will- given some of the things you've told me these past few weeks- I hope you will pay close attention to what happens. It's your life Matt. Don't just have an opinion about the medication, prove to yourself whether your opinion is right or wrong."

"I already said I'd take the pills!" he responded defensively, perhaps because I was implying that I didn't believe the reassurances he gave Dr. Greene and his parents.

"Okay. Sorry if it sounded like I didn't believe you. That wasn't my point. I'm not asking you to tell me what you plan to do. What I am asking is that you pay close attention to what happens if for some reason you toss the pills in the trash."

"I would never do that." Matt said facetiously as his anger evaporated and he smiled. I smiled back and we both laughed no doubt thinking the same thought.

"Hypothetically then, if you do stop taking the medicine, ask yourself these three questions: What stays the same? What gets worse? What gets better? Write it down like we've been doing while you were here. You know what I mean?"

"Yeah. The pluses and minuses."

"Exactly. So you know what I was talking about?"

"Yeah. It's my life I hold the key its up to me to decide."

"Right now you've decided you really don't want to take the medicine. Right?"

"Yeah." he admitted sheepishly. "But I will anyway. Everyone wants me to, so I will."

"Well I don't know if everyone wants you to, but you know my opinion. I hope that you will. But if you decide to stop I want you to know I respect that this is your life and your right."

"Yeah, but you'll think I'm stupid."

"No, I won't. But I might think you made a bad decision if you made an uninformed decision."

"You're the doctor, you would know."

"That's not what I meant. You are in the best position to be the expert on this issue. Be a scientist. Think of this as an experiment. Collect the data. Don't jump to conclusions one way or the other. Just pay attention to what happens when you are not taking the medicine. Ask people you trust how you seem when you're off medicine. Think you'd be interested in doing that?"

"I don't know. I already know the answer."

"Well it seems everyone else already seems to know the answer and most disagree with you. Here's your chance to prove them wrong."

"I'll try to keep an open mind."

"That's all I'm suggesting. Anything else you want to talk about before we stop? Any feedback for me?

"No, I guess not."

"Well, good luck." I stood up, extended my hand and added, "I hope I never see you again."

"Same here." he replied. We both laughed as we shook hands. If I saw Matt, it would be because he was back in the hospital. Keeping him out of the hospital and in his life was something we both wholeheartedly agreed upon.

4. Not React?

Matt was not offering his opinion or saying he would not take his pills. So there was little in the meeting for his doctor and parents to react to. But, his parents were reacting to things Matt had said and done in the past. His father was angry from the start, not only because the hospital was discharging his son who he felt was too ill to come home, but also because he didn't believe that Matt was telling the truth. When Matt said he'd go to his appointment and take his medicine his father reacted by saying, "That's what you promised us before, but when we get home you disappear into your room and you don't go anywhere." Although more subtle, Matt's mother also reacted to his reassurances with disbelief.

There is a time and a place for everything. Sometimes it's important to let our loved one's know how we feel about their actions and statements. But expressing negative feelings to someone with a serious mental illness can feel like you're shouting into their ear with a megaphone. There is actually quite a bit of research on this that you can find out about by using the resources in Chapter 14. The problem has to do with the cognitive deficits caused by these illnesses. A hypersensitivity to the feelings of others is not uncommon. Matt's mother obviously understands this, either by having learned about this aspect of the illness her son has, or by intuition.

5. Let Chaos Be?

Matt was not "talking crazy," so this particular guideline is not so relevant.

6. Echo What They Heard?

No one echoed back to Matt what they understood him to be saying. There was at least one missed opportunity. When Matt said, "this time is different." his doctor or parents could have replied, "how come this time is different. I'd really like to understand that." If such a question had been asked, not with anger or sarcasm, but with genuine curiosity, Matt might have told them something very important because this time really was different for him. He truly did not want to ever come back to the hospital again, certainly not the way he had this time. And if they echoed back what they heard and Matt felt they truly understood, he might have experienced them more as allies than adversaries.

I'll explain. Brian was Matt's doctor, and I was Brian's supervisor, so sometimes I met with the two of them together. During one of these meetings, Matt described the terror he felt when the police brought him to the hospital. He had never felt that scared before. He never wanted to feel that frightened again. And he had grown tired of being hospitalized again and again.

7. Write Down What Matt had to Say?

Writing down what Matt had to say, (e.g., using the ABC in the appendix) would have been awkward in this situation because his doctor and parents never practiced this technique with him. It's true that Brian often took notes during their sessions, but these notations were almost entirely about symptoms he was observing. He rarely recorded Matt's subjective experience of the illness and treatment.

The main reason you want to write down what you've heard is to help you to focus your discussions and so you can better remember your loved one's beliefs about himself, the illness, and treatment. But sometimes you can also use what you have recorded as a tool for improving communication by focusing everyone's attention. I will show you how you can do this in the next example.

Effective Listening

Dr. Ivan Kohut, a third-year resident in psychiatry, was meeting with Vicky, the forty-five-year-old woman with manic depression that I told you about in Chapter 2. Also present was her husband, Scott. Vicky had spent the last three weeks in the hospital following a manic episode during which she took her two children on a three day road-trip to Mount Desert Island National Forest in Maine.

The first night of the trip was especially unusual because Scott had no idea where his family had gone until Vicky called him 11:00 PM. She explained that she wanted their children to experience the same spiritual awakening as her. God had instructed her to take them to the top of Cadillac Mountain, because it was the highest point on the East coast, and that once there he would come to them.

Having survived two previous manic episodes over the course of their marriage, Scott figured out what was happening much more quickly than he had in the past. During the phone call he begged Vicky to come home but she refused, and when he told her he thought she was becoming sick - she abruptly hung up the phone. Scott immediately called the local police who told him there was little they could do other than, "keep an eye out for her car." They suggested he call the Parks Department in Maine. With the help of Vicky's psychiatrist, Scott was able to convince the Park Rangers to intercept his wife when she entered the Park. He flew out to be there, and after much cajoling and threats of commitment, she agreed to return to New York and go to the hospital. From both Scott's and Vicky's perspective the drive back was nightmarish. The children, as children often do, were unconsciously running interference by misbehaving. Their fights and tantrums together with Vicky's rapid-fire speech made for an excruciatingly long drive home.

After greeting the couple, Ivan sat down and began by asking: "What would the two of you like to talk about today? I have two things I'd like to put on our agenda. How about you Vicky?"

"When do I get out of here? That's the only thing I'd like to talk about."

"O.K. Scott, how about you?"

"Well I have the same question. I also want to talk about her medications."

"Anything else? Either of you?"

"No." Vicky answered quickly.

Scott mulled over the question then said "I suppose not, maybe more will occur to me as we talk."

"Good. My two agenda items are similar. I want to report on how I think Vicky is doing and on the discharge plan. So that's basically three items: 1.) The plan for discharge; 2.) Medications; and 3.) Where we're at right now. If it's OK with the two of you, I'd like to get the last item out of the way." Vicky and Scott both nodded their approval. "I think you are doing much better than when we first met three weeks ago." Ivan said addressing Vicky. "Back then you were sleeping about 2 to 4 hours a night, your thoughts were racing, your speech was pressured, you were euphoric, extremely irritable, and had some unusual thoughts about God and about supernatural abilities you felt he had given you. Right now your sleep is back to normal, your thoughts aren't racing, and your speech isn't pressured. You don't need me to describe your mood. How would you describe your mood over the last week?"

"Kind of constricted. I'm not as happy and I don't get irritated so easily. I'm not depressed."

"Do you miss the happy feeling?"

"You know I do Dr. Kohut! Wouldn't you?"

"Absolutely." Noting the smile on her face he added "But it looks to me like you can still feel happy. It's the extreme happiness, the high, that's gone. Yes?"

"That's true." she answered.

"So, in a nutshell, I think you're ready to go home the day after next."

Vicky looked surprised and said "Well, that answers my question. Why didn't you tell me that this morning when we met?"

"I suppose you don't remember, but I told you that I had to discuss it with the Team first. I wanted everyone's input and we generally make these decisions by consensus. And the consensus is that you're much improved and can go home. Scott, any opinion about this?"

"Not really. I expected it. I see that she's getting back to normal. But I guess I am not clear on what happens next? What about the medications and what can we do to keep this from happening again?"

"Good segue way to the last thing on our agenda. What happens next with respect to your treatment." Ivan answered, addressing Vicky once again. "I'd like to see you in the clinic once a week for the next couple of months, and then, maybe drop down to once a month. I don't want to change anything about the medication you're taking right now. I'd like to see how you do over the next couple of weeks then re-evaluate and discuss if we should make any adjustments. What are your thoughts about what should happen next?"

Vicky laughed and asked, "Does it really matter? Everyone thinks I should stay on medication."

"Of course it matters!" Scott replied, a little irritated and defensive.

"You're the boss here - even if it doesn't seem that way now." Ivan added.

"What are you talking about?" Vicky asked.

"I am talking about the fact that what your husband and I think you should do doesn't amount to a hill of beans next to what *you* think you should do. If you believe that the medications have done their job and want to stop - you will. I can't stop you and neither can your husband."

"Then why am I in this hospital? I don't feel like the boss."

"That's because you lost a lot of control when the bipolar disorder you have flared up. It caused you to do things that worried a lot of people and motivated them to take control away from you. But you've got the illness under control again and you're back in the driver's seat."

"If that's true, then I don't want to take these drugs for more than a month or two."

"That's your choice..."

"Wait a minute!" Scott interrupted, "That's how she got into this mess in the first place. Every doctor she's seen, including you, have told us she will very likely have to stay on these medications for the rest of her life."

"If she doesn't want to have another flare-up - that's true. Also, the medications will help to keep her from becoming depressed again. I am not contradicting myself. I am saying something different. It's Vicky's choice - not yours or mine. But the choices you make," he added now addressing Vicky, "will have consequences."

"You make it sound so ominous." she replied.

"I think the consequences of stopping your treatment will be very negative. You know what my professional recommendation is and what your last psychiatrist felt. You know what your husband and your family would like. But what you believe is what you will ultimately do. But I am curious about one thing. Why don't you think you will need them? Just this morning you told me they've been very helpful over the past few weeks. Were you just 'yessing' me or did you really mean it?"

"I meant it. They've done their job. But I am better now."

"So you see yourself as cured of bipolar disorder." Ivan stated.

"Yes. And that's the main reason I don't want to be on these drugs for the rest of my life."

"That's not necessarily impossible." Ivan said to the couples' surprise, "How about we make a deal. If you decide, six months from now, that you still want to go off your medications, we can give it a try. But I won't have any part of it if we're not meeting regularly."

"Why would you do that? You already told me you think I have to stay on these forever."

"Because your opinion is the only one that ultimately determines whether or not you stay in treatment. I am willing to work with you to prove what you believe even though I don't believe it. I have only two requirements; that you see me regularly and that you keep a daily diary during the time we are lowering your dosages."

"Why a diary?"

"So you have a record of how you were thinking and acting during the time your medication was lowered. It will also help you to pay attention to the consequences. Not only for you, but for your family."

Vicky replied, "I would be willing to do that."

"O.K. Lets write the deal down so we all remember. You will stay on the medications for another six months. If at that time you still want to discontinue the drugs, we do it together." he said aloud as he wrote down his words. Then he added as an afterthought, "I'd like to include Scott in some of those meetings as well if that's OK?"

"Sure." she answered.

"And if we go that route you will keep a daily diary. We can talk more about what I'd like you to record - cross that bridge when we come to it. Do I have it right? Is this what we agreed to?"

"Yes," both Vicky and Scott replied.

Lets review the seven listening guidelines I gave above. Did Dr. Kohut and Vicky's husband:

1. Set Aside the Time?
Yes.

2. Agree on an Agenda?
Not only did they agree on an agenda, but over the course of their conversation Ivan repeatedly checked back with Vicky and her husband to insure that there wasn't any more either of them wanted to talk about. Also, the agenda was highly relevant to what was foremost in Vicky's mind.

3. Listen for Beliefs about the Self and the Illness?
Ivan clearly had been listening when they talked previously because he referred back to Vicky's beliefs about not needing to take medication. He confirmed that she still felt this way and then asked her to tell him why she believed she would no longer require medication. What was her rationale? She felt that the medications were a short-term treatment. Like antibiotics for an infection, rather than a long-term treatment like insulin for diabetes.

4. Not React?
Both Ivan and Scott did not react emotionally to

Vicky's statement that she wanted to stop taking medication. Scott listened and Ivan asked her to explain further. Ivan didn't immediately jump in with his opinion as a counter point to Vicky's statement that she planned to stop taking the medication.

5. Let Chaos Be?

Vicky's speech and ideas were well organized so this guideline was not needed.

6. Echo What They Heard?

Ivan did this repeatedly, often rephrasing things Vicky had said to insure that he "got it right."

7. Write it Down?

Ivan not only wrote down what they had agreed to do about the medications, but asked permission to do so before starting. This was important because it further emphasized Ivan's wish to collaborate rather than pontificate. By asking, he underscored that Vicky was in charge after she left the hospital. He wasn't afraid to acknowledge his own powerlessness. By doing so, he reminded Vicky that the choice to continue treatment was hers as was the responsibility for the consequences that followed her decision.

Summary

Listening is an active process. It involves asking many questions and not reacting to what you are hearing. You should think of yourself as a scientist trying to unravel a mystery. Your task is to gain a clear idea of what *your loved one's* experience of the illness and treatment is. Once you know how he experiences the idea of having a mental illness and taking psychiatric drugs you will have acquired vital knowledge that you need to build a treatment agreement.

Chapter 7
Empathize

A few years after he first became ill, my brother and I were talking about one of his medications, Haldol. He hated Haldol because it made him feel "stiff" and sleepy. He also hated the lithium he was taking, but was less precise about the reason. He could live with the Cogentin, he told me, although he wasn't sure what it was doing for him. As I listened to his complaints, I understood for the first time since he became ill some of the frustration he felt about taking these medications. I recall saying, "I can see why you don't like these drugs. It sounds like they make you feel really uncomfortable and groggy." The conversation stands out in my mind because for the first time in a long time we were listening to one another and not arguing.

Usually our conversations on the topic of medication were pedantic. I would hold my ground and pontificate about why he must take the medications prescribed for him and about his immaturity for not accepting the fact that he was ill. Brothers can often be that way. But with a year under my belt as a therapy aide

Empathy ultimately resulted in my brother showing a real interest in my thoughts about the illness he felt he did not have and, the medications he was sure he did not need.

on an inpatient psychiatric ward, I knew how important it was to listen. As I listened, I couldn't help but begin to empathize. I love Henry, and when someone you love is in pain, it's hard not to empathize. Learning to listen led to empathy. And empathy ultimately resulted in my brother showing a real interest in *my thoughts* about the illness he felt he did not have and the medications he was sure he did not need.

When you feel empathy and convey it, your loved one will very likely feel understood and respected. Whenever you convey that you understand how your loved one is feeling, his defensiveness will decrease and openness to alternative ways of thinking will increase. If you have done your homework, if you have listened carefully to your loved one's experience of his illness and the prescribed treatment, you will naturally begin to empathize. But communicating your empathy is not always so natural. In fact, for many people it feels awkward at first. In this chapter, you will learn how to better convey your empathy and to recognize when defenses have been lowered, giving you an opening to connect with your loved one. Your ultimate goal is to create a window of opportunity for you to begin forming a treatment agreement.

Conveying empathy

You must first learn what it is with which you should be empathizing. The short answer is just about any feeling your loved one is willing to reveal. But there are certain feelings that are particularly important for you to understand. Here is a list of the most common and relevant feelings below.

Whether the feelings expressed are rational ("I am so sick and tired of everybody telling me I am sick!") or irrational ("The C.I.A. has implanted microchips in the capsules so they can track me!"), you want to be sure to empathize with:

- **Frustrations** (about pressure from others to take medication and about personal goals that have not been met).

- **Fears** (about medication, being stigmatized, and failing).

- **Discomfort** (attributed to medications such as gaining weight, or feeling groggy, slowed down, less creative, stiff, etc.).

- **Desires** (to work, get married, have children, return to school, stay out of the hospital, etc.).

Below is an example of what to empathize with and how to do it. One technique I illustrate, called reflective listening, is vital to the task of forming a treatment agreement.

Dolores

Dolores, who has had schizophrenia for nearly 20 years, told me that she didn't need medication or a day treatment program because there was nothing wrong with her. What did Dolores feel she needed? More than anything else, she wanted a job. She was frustrated that she did not have a job and with her family who told her she couldn't work. Her family was being reasonably pessimistic. The fact is that Dolores had been unable to keep a job for more than a few days at a time and that she had been employed only a handful of times over the past twenty years.

I met Dolores during her most recent hospitalization. Like many individuals with serious mental illness who don't know they're ill, Dolores had been hospitalized many times; in her case, about two to four times a year. Although she almost always agreed to sign herself into the hospital voluntarily, she would do this only after receiving tremendous pressure from her family. When talking with her about what she planned to do when she left the hospital, she told me simply, "Get a job."

If you were her therapist and discussing her plans after discharge from the hospital, you might be tempted (as I was early in my career) to focus on the irrationality of Dolores' plan for herself. There was no reason to believe that her long-standing pattern of unemployment was about to change. You might be further tempted to go that route because Dolores had an equally long history of poor adherence to her medication regimen. You would understandably think that a discussion about her reluctance to stay in treatment would be more beneficial to her. But she wasn't interested in talking about drugs, day treatment programs, or doctor's appointments. So I began our talk about her plans for the future by empathizing with what she was feeling that moment.

"You want to get a job when you leave. Do you have a plan?"

"I'm going to work on Wall Street," she answered quickly.

"Why Wall Street?" I asked, ignoring for now how far-fetched her plan was.

"I want to make a lot of money. I need to have my own money."

"It's important to you to have your own money." I reflected back to her.

"Yes. I hate having to ask my family for money."

"How come?"

"It makes me feel like a child. My little sister [who was in her thirties] is a stockbroker and you should see her house. I'm the big sister; I should be making money too!"

"It sounds like it makes you feel embarrassed or even a little humiliated. Am I right about that?" I asked, checking to see if I understood her feelings and at the same time communicating my empathy.

"It does. Wouldn't you be embarrassed?" she asked.

"Yes, I think I probably would feel that way." Sensing an opening, I added, "Can I ask you something?"

"What?"

Careful not to add to her humiliation and raise her defenses, I asked, "Why do you think you haven't worked very much?" (instead of, "Why is it you've only worked about twelve days in your entire adult life?"). She quickly answered "Because I'm always in the damn hospital!"

"You're frustrated about being in the hospital so much?"

"No, I'm angry about being in the hospital so much. I want to get on with my life and I can't if I'm in a damn hospital."

"So it's much more than frustration you feel. It makes you angry. Yes?" I asked, nodding my head.

"Very angry," she answered more calmly.

Pushing ahead, I asked, "How do you feel about the fact that it's been hard to find work?"

"Sometimes I want to scream!"

"Sounds very frustrating. Is it?"

"It is frustrating," she answered.

During this brief exchange, I empathized with Dolores' feelings of *humiliation*, her deep *desire* to work, and her *frustration* with being unable to work. Did you notice that nearly everything I said was in the form of a question? This technique is called reflective listening. It's an active form of listening that involves restating, in the form of a question, your understanding of what you just heard. When I said "Sounds very frustrating. Is it?" I was using reflective listening. By making a statement about my understanding of her feelings and asking if I had it right, I was able to check if I understood what she meant when she said she wanted to scream. I also communicated my empathy for what she was feeling. Go back and reread our discussion looking for instances of reflective listening. It is a vital skill to learn if you want to achieve *your* goals.

By asking questions instead of commenting on what she had to say ("What you're planning isn't realistic."), I learned about what was important to Dolores, what was foremost on her mind, and how she was feeling. More important, I communicated my understanding of how it felt by reflecting back any statements she made about how she was feeling. This created a window of opportunity that I used later to discuss what role, if any, she felt treatment might play in what she wanted to accomplish.

Summary

Whenever you want to facilitate change in another person, you must first find out what motivates him; what goals and feelings are driving his behavior? Whenever you convey empathy for anther person's experience, he feels understood and respected. Because you understand the other person's point of view and how they feel about it, there is nothing to argue about. Consequently, defensiveness goes down and openness to hearing your perspective increases. Here are some main points to remember about empathy:

1.   **Empathy creates windows of opportunity** for change by lowering defenses and communicating respect for the other person's point of view.

2.   **Show your empathy for:**

   • **frustrations** (about pressure from others to take medication and about personal goals that have not been met.);
   • **fears** (about medication, being stigmatized, and failing);
   • **discomfort** (attributed to medications, such as gaining weight or feeling groggy, slowed down, less creative, stiff, etc.); and
   • **desires** (to work, get married, have children, return to school, stay out of the hospital, be normal, etc.).

3. Convey your empathy by using reflective listening.
      Reflective listening involves reflecting back statements about feelings in the form of questions. By using this technique, you clarify what it is the other person is feeling and convey your interest in understanding her experience and point of view.
      In the following chapter, you will learn how to use the window of opportunity your empathy creates and how to communicate your beliefs about the illness and treatment to set the stage for change.

Chapter 8
Agree

Having listened carefully to your loved one's attitudes and feelings about treatment, and having conveyed your empathy, you have undoubtedly found areas where the two of you agree. I never shared Matt's beliefs that God had chosen him as his special messenger to world leaders or that the CIA was trying to assassinate him, nor his conviction he was not ill. But we did agree on at least one thing: that it was very important to keep him out of the hospital. Dolores and I agreed on something similar, and on her goal of getting a job. Although I didn't think it was likely that work was right around the corner for her, I did believe she could start taking some steps in that direction. Vicky and Dr. Kohut agreed to examine together, whether she truly needed to take medication when out of the hospital. My brother and I have agreed for a long time now that when he takes his medication regularly he stays out of the hospital, the voices he hears diminish and bother him less, he becomes less fearful, and he is less likely to be asked to leave the coffee houses he likes to frequent.

Whenever you see a window of opportunity to convey your observations and opinions, always begin with something your loved one already acknowledges and believes.

Whenever you see a window of opportunity to convey your observations and opinions, always begin with something your loved one already acknowledges and believes. The more common ground you can find, the better. When you share the same goals, you can work together instead of at odds. Lets look at how to recognize and use a window of opportunity to find common ground.

Recognizing and using windows of opportunity

Dolores believes the main reason she had not been able to find work was because of her frequent hospitalizations. Although this was certainly part of the reason (you can't work and be in the hospital at the same time), it was the end product of what I believed to be more relevant factors. She had very little insight into the more salient reasons she had trouble finding and holding onto a job.

According to her family, Dolores had lost the few jobs that she was able to get because of the symptoms of her illness. For example, she would begin talking to herself while at work, having quiet conversations with the voices she was hearing. Sometimes, she would become paranoid of her bosses and co-workers and accuse them of plotting against her.

I avoided the issue of symptoms or the role that they played in her being fired. Instead, I focused on the other part of her explanation that we did agree upon.

Dolores didn't recognize the symptoms of her illness, much less the role they played in keeping her unemployed. Instead, she felt her numerous stays in the hospital were causing the problem. Consequently, when we talked about her desire to work, I avoided the issue of symptoms or the role they played in her being fired (unless she specifically asked my opinion about this issue). Instead, I focused on the part of her explanation that we did agree upon. Hospitalizations. I agreed with her that being in the hospital made it impossible for her to work. This led to our agreeing on something else that helped me to formulate a treatment agreement she could accept. Before telling you more about Dolores, I want to tell you about six things that I try to do whenever I see a window of opportunity. When defenses have been lowered and your loved one appears receptive to hearing your views:

1. **Normalize the experience** ("I would feel the same were if I was in your shoes.").

2. **Discuss only perceived problems/symptoms** (Statements such as, "I can't sleep at night because I'm constantly on guard. I am so afraid that they're going to come and hurt me," describe insomnia and paranoia stemming from a delusion. However, the words insomnia and delusion need not ever be used in your discussions).

3. **Review perceived advantages and disadvantages of treatment** (whether rational or irrational).

4. **Correct misconceptions** (antipsychotic medications are not addictive; serious mental illness is not caused by one's upbringing or use of illicit drugs).

5. **Reflect back and highlight the perceived benefits** ("So if I have it right, you're saying that when you stay on the medication you sleep better and you fight less with your family?").

6. **Agree to disagree** (whenever areas of disagreement are brought to the surface).

Dolores was angry and frustrated about being hospitalized so frequently and with how this interfered with her goal of getting a job. I empathized with her frustration and anger when I asked, "It sounds like you feel really frustrated about being in the hospital again."

"Very. I need to get out of the hospital and get back to work. I'm going to go crazy if I stay here much longer."

"You're feeling stir crazy?"

"Yes!"

I followed with, "You know something? We're exactly the same that way. I would go absolutely stir-crazy if I were locked up in a hospital and didn't have a job. In fact, I think anyone would feel that way."

With this small bit of self-revelation I was helping to *normalize the experience* Dolores was having. I then asked her if there were any other reasons she was not having luck holding down a job. Some of her ideas made sense, others were illogical, if not frankly delusional, and scattered in between were little kernels of insight into how her disorganized behavior may have contributed to being fired repeatedly.

Noting these instances of insight, I then asked her if she wanted my thoughts on *her problem* (notice that we are now talking about a problem *she perceives* she has). She did.

I began by reflecting back, what she had said earlier and then asked a question, "Well certainly being in the hospital is interfering with work. I guess that raises the question of what you can do to stay out of the hospital?"

"I don't know. Move away from my family?" she answered wryly.

"Is there any pattern that you've noticed?"

"Well my father is usually the first one to start picking fights with me. He tells me I'm sick and need to go to the hospital. He's always on my back about taking my medications."

"Why is that?"

"He thinks I'm psycho."

"That bothers you?"

"Yeah it bothers me."

"I can see why that bothers you. 'Psycho' is a pretty derogatory label to use. Does he actually say that? Does he say you're 'psycho,' or is that how it feels to you?"

"No, he doesn't say it. He thinks I have a chemical imbalance in my brain." Here I am normalizing her experience by acknowledging that being called a 'psycho' would be bothersome, to say the least, to most anyone. It is a derogatory term. I am also asking for clarification.

"So if you were taking your medications you think he wouldn't be on your back?"

"I know he wouldn't."

"I see. And when the two of you fight about the medication it often ends up with you going to the hospital?"

"I have to, just to get some peace."

"So would it be fair to say that there are two advantages to taking your medications? The first being that your father would not be 'on your back' and the second benefit is that you would be less likely to go to the hospital?"

"Yes."

"Yes what?" I asked her to clarify to determine exactly what it was she was agreeing to.

"If I took my pills my father would leave me alone and I wouldn't have to come here."

"What are some of the disadvantages to taking medications?" I followed quickly, as she seemed reluctant to acknowledge the two advantages I had identified.

"I am not a psycho, for one. Also, I hate how much weight I gain whenever I'm on them."

"What else? Are there other side effects or other things about the drugs that you see as a disadvantage?"

"They make me hear voices. And besides, I don't want to get addicted."

"You are worried about getting addicted?"

"Yes. These are powerful mind-altering drugs."

"They're powerful and they do affect the way you think and feel. Would you like to hear about my experience with the drugs you're taking?"

"You've taken these!?" she asked incredulously.

"Well, not the drugs you're taking now. But over the years I have seen more people than I can count who have taken these medications. My professional experience leads me to the conclusion that the drugs you are taking are *not* addictive and they *don't* cause voices like the ones you hear."

"How do you know?"

"From talking to people who have taken these drugs and from reading the research."

"I always thought they were addictive."

"Well, they're not. At least I've never seen it. Do you still want to put on the list that 'they cause you to hear voices' and they're 'addictive'?"

"No, I guess not."

"Your call," I said, pausing to see if she was going to change her mind. Then continued, "Any other disadvantages to taking medication?"

"It's embarrassing. I don't want people to know."

"Can we write this down so I can keep track?" I asked, wanting to record together, rather than alone afterward, the advantages and disadvantages Dolores and I were identifying.

"Sure."

Taking out a pad and pen, I asked, "What were the disadvantages again?"

"They make me feel like I'm psycho, they're embarrassing, and I gain weight."

"And the advantages were what?"

"My father isn't on my back and I stay out of the hospital."

I read the list back to her to make sure that I had it correct and asked her to keep thinking about the advantages and disadvantages of taking medication.

"Why should I keep thinking about it? You're like everyone. You want me to take these drugs just like my father," she reacted defensively.

"No, that's not my reason for asking you to keep thinking about it. You have never really asked me my opinion about what I think you should do about medications after leaving the hospital. While you are here, I have been clear that I think you should take them. But you haven't asked me what I think you should do afterward. Besides, we weren't really talking about medications. We were talking about your getting a job and how being in the hospital keeps you from your goal."

Dolores visibly relaxed as I spoke and said, "So you don't think I should take the medications after I leave?"

"No, I didn't say that. I said you've never really asked me my opinion."

"So what's your opinion?"

"Well, if we are talking about your goal of getting a job, then I see the same two advantages that you see. Your father will be less bothersome and you'll stay out of the hospital. So those are two good reasons to take them. I also see three reasons not to take them. You gain weight, they make you feel like you're a psycho, as you put it, and you feel embarrassed about taking the pills."

"So what's your opinion?"

"I'll tell you if you want, but I think the more important question right now, at least in my mind, is whether you think the advantages outweigh the disadvantages?"

"I'm not sure," she answered slowly.

"So don't you think its worth keeping track of? You know, what is good versus what is bad about taking the medications. Because it sounds like when you don't it creates a lot of conflict at home and you end up in the hospital."

"I guess so."

"Did I answer your question about what my opinion is?" I asked, making sure that I wasn't being perceived as dodging the bullet, and to create another opportunity to go over the pluses and minuses of medication.

"Yes. You think I should take them if I want my father off my back and want to stay out of the hospital."

"That's basically right, except you said it would help with your father and ultimately keep you out of the hospital, not me. I said it was important to try and keep track of the pluses and minuses. I also said that I know there are things about taking the medication that you don't like." I added this comment to emphasize the fact that I hadn't lost sight of the negatives.

During another conversation, I had an opportunity to add another benefit to the list we had started. I should mention I never met with her again without bringing the list we had begun. Prior to this conversation, I did a little homework. Since Dolores was on a research unit that made a point of tracking down and obtaining copies of old medical records. This is something that almost never happens when someone who is seriously mentally ill is hospitalized. The exceptions are due to family members or therapists keeping copies of the medical records themselves which they then duplicate and give to hospital staff. I looked for periods of time when she was hospitalized and compared these instances to times she was employed. I was not surprised to find that instances when she was able to work corresponded to periods when she was taking her medication faithfully. I asked her if she wanted to hear about what I thought might be another benefit, "I think there may be another benefit to taking medication that's not on our list. Want to hear what it is?"

"O.K."

"I was looking over your medical records and discovered an interesting pattern. You were not taking medication almost every time you lost a job. Have you noticed that pattern?"

"No," she answered quickly.

"You answered that kind of fast. Can I suggest something?"

"What?"

"Just think about it some more. Not now. Later. See if you can remember whether you were taking medications when you had the job and whether you and your father were arguing a lot during those times. Can you do that?"

"I can do that. I'll think about it."

"In the meantime, can I add it to our list with a question mark? A possible benefit?"

"Sure. But I don't think its true."

"I know. But I think it is. We don't have to agree on this. In fact, lets agree to disagree!"

"I agree that you're wrong!" she answered with a big grin on her face.

"But you'll keep an open mind to the possibility that I am right and I'll do the same. I'll stay open to the possibility that you are right. Agreed?"

"Agreed," she answered, serious again.

During our conversations, I tried very hard to follow the six guidelines given above. Whenever possible, I tried to *normalize her experience*, usually by letting her know that if I were in her shoes I would likely feel the same way (about being hospitalized, being called a 'psycho,' taking medication). I was very careful to *discuss only those problems (and symptoms) Dolores mentioned herself.* And I took every opportunity I could find to *review the advantages and disadvantages of treatment.* Here as well, I was careful to only discuss the pluses and minuses Dolores had raised herself.

The one time I told her of an advantage she had not identified herself, I first asked if she wanted to hear my opinion ("I think there may be another benefit to taking medication that's not on our list. Want to hear what it is?"). Remember to always ask questions whenever you

> *Remember to always ask questions whenever you want to make a point. By couching your opinion in a question, you emphasize that you want to collaborate and not pontificate.*

want to make a point. By couching your opinion in a question, you emphasize that you want to collaborate and not pontificate.

When we spoke, I kept my eyes peeled for any misconceptions Dolores held about medication. I *corrected her mistaken belief* that the medications she was taking caused hallucinations and were addictive. Then I asked her if she still wanted to put these complaints on the list. If she had said yes, I would have complied, but I would have also asked her if we could revisit the issue later.

I *reflected back (repeated) and highlighted the benefits* she mentioned whenever the opportunity presented itself. And we *agreed to disagree* about whether or not Dolores had stopped taking medications prior to losing her jobs. I encourage you to go back and reread our discussions to see if you can identify when I used each guideline.

Summary

From a position of empathy, you can help your loved one to feel more normal and amplify those beliefs that are relevant to arriving at a treatment agreement. Make and keep a list of the advantages and disadvantages to staying in treatment (drugs, psychotherapy, day programs, occupational therapy, etc.).

Be careful to always list any negatives that are mentioned. It increases your credibility and flags potential obstacles to arriving at a treatment agreement.

Correct misconceptions about treatment whenever you can and highlight any benefits your loved one already experiences. Finally, whenever an area of disagreement is revealed, try and agree to disagree. Whenever this happens, mutual respect for each other's opinion is conveyed and openness to being proven wrong is more likely. This is vital if your loved one is to reconsider their stance on staying in treatment. Don't be afraid to say that you might also be wrong. If you're not open to being proven wrong, why should your loved one be?

Chapter 9
Partnership

"How did the psychologist find his wife who was lost in the woods...? He followed the psycho-path." Henry Amador, October 1997

Henry and I both agreed that being hospitalized was something to be avoided. We also agreed on his goal of getting a job and of obtaining more "pocket money" so he could buy soft drinks, cigarettes, or a hamburger if he felt like it. Although I felt he was much further away from holding down a job then he did, this difference in opinion was very rarely mentioned. And when I did mention it, it was only when he cornered me. ("You don't think I can work right now, do you?"). Instead, I made a point of talking with him, whenever the opportunity presented itself, about what it would take for him to achieve that goal.

It took some time, but we both agreed that when he took his medication he stayed out of the hospital. At first he attributed the relationship between taking his pills and not being hospitalized to a reduction in the pressure he was getting to stay on the medication rather than any benefit derived from the drugs. In other words, he knew if he stayed on the medication his doctor and family would not force the issue of hospitalization. In time, however, he came to see his medication as helpful in other ways.

Today, if you were to ask him why he takes the medication he would tell you "It helps me with the voices and it makes me less paranoid." Over the past few years I have noticed that he tells people that he has " schizoaffective disorder."

His awareness of how medication helped him, and his insight into having a serious mental illness, grew out of the partnerships he developed with various therapists and with me. We often spoke about his fervent desire to get a job. Whenever we did, I empathized with his frustration and encouraged him to try to figure out why he could not keep the jobs he found.

My guess is that he has worked in more than a dozen twenty-four hour convenience stores over the past 15 years. Most stints were for a week at most, ending with his being fired or simply not showing up for work anymore.

He had various explanations that I listened to attentively and without challenging their irrationality. Whenever I asked him if I could tell him what I thought, and he said yes, I kept raising the same hypothesis "Whatever else might be happening," I would tell him, "it's hard to work when you're feeling anxious and hearing voices." Henry knew the medications "blocked the voices" and helped him "feel less paranoid." But he had yet to make the link to how this interfered with his ability to hold down a job.

> *Try to agree on goals that are reachable whenever you can.*

I can't say for certain how much this observation added to his developing the high level of adherence to treatment he currently has. But I am sure it helped the cause, at least a little. I know this because he wouldn't argue with me as he had in the past, probably because I never wanted to argue about such things anymore and also because I couched my opnion in a "hypothesis." I didn't tell him what the problem was. Instead, I gave him my best guess. Instead of being defensive, he would listen to my hypothesis and take it in. He was at least considering the possibility I was correct.

Regardless of the fact he has taken his medication more consistently for the past five years, he still hasn't reached his goal of holding down a job. This highlights an important point. Try to agree on reachable goals whenever you can.

Fortunately, when it came to his goal of obtaining some spending money, I was able to provide him with an opportunity for success. Each business day I sent him a check for five dollars, care of his therapist at the day program in which he was enrolled. When I began doing this I worked out a contract with Henry and his case-worker regarding the things he needed to do in order for the money to be released to him. The main task was to attend

He felt insulted by my proposal and I realized that our partnership was in jeopardy of reverting to estrangement. So I stopped and talked with him about his feelings and empathized with his anger and frustration.

the program. The other requirement was that he not be belligerent and hostile when money was withheld for the days that he missed (he had penchant for this behavior when he did not get what he wanted).

At first he felt angry and that I was treating him like an infant. He felt insulted by my proposal and I realized our partnership was in jeopardy of reverting to estrangement. So I stopped and talked with him about his feelings and empathized with his anger and frustration.

I also apologized for having an opinion that differed from his. He felt that if I loved him I should give him the money regardless of whether he went to the day program or not. Furthermore, he wanted me to send the full amount weekly, rather than dolling it out five dollars at a time. I told him his attendance at the program was so important to his well-being that I wanted to give him an extra incentive to do it. I also said I worried about what he would do with the money if I sent larger amounts directly to him. He felt bribed and I struggled with feeling guilty.

Our treatment agreement consisted of two main elements: he agreed to take his medication (to help him to stay out of the hospital) and to go to his day program every day (so he could have spending money).

But I stuck to my guns explaining, "I really want to help you out. I want to give you this money. But if you are not going to the program, or at least checking in with them everyday, I worry that things are going to go downhill and you'll end up in the hospital again." I added I thought I might actually worsen things for him if I sent him the money directly. My brother can be very impulsive with money. Often he gives it away to people in need, hits the road hitchhiking, or spends it on beer (which he can't drink without causing an exacerbation of the illness). He didn't think I should have these concerns. But he did understand that, right or wrong, these were things that worried me greatly. We ultimately agreed to disagree. But in the process we found something we could agree on. Henry suggested a compromise. Rather than go to the program for the entire day, he would go in the morning to pick up his check and spend a few minutes talking with his caseworker. His suggestion immediately made sense to me because I knew my brother found the program tiresome and boring. He felt everyone there was worse off than him. No doubt, many of his peers felt the same way. I can't say that I blame him. I would also find the program he was in at the time excruciatingly boring. I understood his perspective and he knew it. In the end we agreed he would go every day to pickup the check and spend a few minutes talking with his caseworker about the previous day. To my surprise, I learned that once he got there he often stayed for several hours.

Our treatment agreement consisted of two main elements: he agreed to take his medication (to help him to stay out of the hospital) and go to his day program everyday (so he could have spending money). In the past five years he has been hospitalized about five times. Always voluntarily and always for very short stays (usually a few days). I doubt anyone can provide an accurate accounting of the number of hospitalizations he had prior to this period of time. I know for certain he averaged about four hospitalizations per year, each lasting a couple of weeks or longer.

Many other unexpected benefits grew out of us forming a partnership and treatment agreement. Our respect for one another grew as did our comfort with spending time together. I truly enjoy spending time with him now. He makes me laugh and feel very loved. I think I do the same for him.

Matt

Matt formed similar partnerships and treatment agreements. Matt and his parents agreed it was very important to try to keep him out of the hospital and to reduce the high level of conflict they had at home.

> *They abandoned the approach of confronting their son with the fact of his illness in favor of a more practical method.*

Mr. and Mrs. Blackburn decided to meet with me after the hospitalization I first told you about in Chapter 3. Our discussions centered on helping them to develop the listening skills and techniques I described in Chapters 5 through 10. I also directed them to the local chapter of the National Alliance for the Mentally Ill, where they learned of resources in their area and received free literature about their son's illness. Mr. and Mrs. Blackburn were quick to see the benefits of the approach I suggested. They were tired of fighting with their son and sorely needed a break from all the hostility that had built up between them over the years. They abandoned the approach of confronting their son with his illness in favor of a more practical method. They listened and learned that Matt wanted to stay out of the hospital as much as they did and he also wished desperately for peace at home. The peace emerged naturally as the Blackburn's backed off from trying to convince their son he was ill. It took about two months, but Matt slowly began to listen and to understand how his parents felt about his medication.

He felt badly that his mother became very frightened when he was not taking medication. If you recall what Matt was like at home and how he felt about taking medication, this may sound a little far fetched. But Matt's guilt emerged from many discussions with his parents, mostly his mother, during which they never once told him what he should do.

They asked questions and when he asked them what they thought, they gave their opinion along with the acknowledgment that they could be wrong. They didn't think it was likely they were wrong about why he needed to take medication, but they could consider the possibility.

When his mother told him he frightened her when he stopped taking medication he felt bad. For this reason and because his parents said there was a good possibility they might not be able to live with him any longer if he did not take the medicine, Matt agreed the benefits to taking the medicine far outweighed the disadvantages. This did not happen overnight. It took a couple of months, but it resulted in Matt and his parents accomplishing both goals they had set out to achieve. I received a card from the Blackburns over the holidays last year. Under Mrs. Blackburn's graceful penmanship that conveyed the family's good wishes for the new year her husband had scrawled a little note: "Thanks again for your help. Matt has not been in the hospital in over a year!"

Dolores

Dolores and I agreed on something similar to what the Blackburns had agreed upon, and on her goal of getting a job. Although I didn't think it was likely work was right around the corner for her, I did believe she could start taking some steps in that direction. Like with my brother, I looked for opportunities to share my hypothesis that she may need to be on medication to keep a job. As you may recall, I once asked her to keep an open mind about this possibility. She didn't think I was correct and we *agreed to disagree* about whether or not Dolores had stopped taking medications prior to losing her jobs. But she accepted my suggestion that she be a scientist and keep an open mind. During her next hospitalization, just five months after the last, we had an opportunity to discuss my theory again. I began by asking her if she had kept the list of advantages and disadvantages to taking medication that we had started when she was in the hospital the last time. She didn't know where it was. But since I put a copy in her medical record, we were able to go over it again. Her current assessment of the pros and cons to taking medication was consistent with her previous one. When we got to my note about work that was under the advantages column with a question mark, I asked her "When you were here last you were planning on getting a job when you left. Any luck?"

"Yes. I got a job as a cashier at the grocery store near me."

"That's good news. Congratulations. How has it been going?"

"He fired me."

"Who fired you?" I asked.

"The manager. He said I talked too much."

"Can I ask you about whether you were taking your medication at the time?"

"No. I stopped. I didn't need it anymore." Showing her the list I had kept I asked her if she remembered why I put a question mark behind the word "work" in the advantages column.

"We disagreed about that. I was supposed to think about it."

"What do you think?" I couldn't help but ask.

"Its true I wasn't taking the medication, but I don't know if that had anything to do with it."

"O.K., shall we make a note of it anyway?" I asked.

"I don't care, sure, go ahead."

"Can you keep an open mind to the possibility that medication helps you to work?"

"Yes," she answered definitively.

Dolores was hospitalized again about three months later and although she had not found a job in the interim we talked about the issue again. She was more open to the idea and admitted that when she stopped taking the medication she talked to herself more. Her family said that one of the problems she had at work was talking to the voices she heard whenever she was off medication. This led to a discussion of how other people might view her talking aloud to herself when she was checking them out at the grocery store. She said, "They's think I was nuts!" Having made this link I tried for another and asked her whether she was hearing voices and talking to herself the last time she was fired. Again, she answered yes.

It took three hospitalizations and encouragement from her family and outpatient psychiatrist, but Dolores finally agreed that taking medication would very likely help her to work. Now everyone was on board with the idea and her psychiatrist and parents focused on reminding her of this advantage (that she believed in) rather than try and get her to understand she had an illness and needed medication. I should note that Dolores agreed to take her medication even though she still did not think she was ill.

Dolores was not hospitalized again for nearly twenty months. With the help of her family, she was able to get her job back at the grocery store with the explicit agreement that taking medication was a prerequisite. Dolores was lucky that the store manager had some personal experience with mental illness in his family and wanted to help out.

Vicky

Vicky lowered her medication dosage six months after her hospitalization. As you may recall she believed that once she was out of the hospital she would no longer need the medicine. She agreed with Dr. Kohut that she would stay on the medicine for at least six months and if she still wanted to try to go off she would do it under her doctor's supervision.

She was seeing Dr. Kohut weekly as they had agreed, and her husband was aware of what she was doing. Dr. Kohut asked Vicky and her husband Scott to keep a daily diary to record a description of her mood, speech and thinking. They were asked to note if any of the symptoms Vicky had insight into (grandiosity, euphoria, insomnia, and pressured speech), were returning. After two weeks on a lowered dose of lithium, Vicky reported she was sleeping less and not feeling tired. She also said that Scott felt she was getting "hyper" and talking more than usual. When I asked her if she agreed with Scott's observation, she reluctantly said yes.

The experiment lasted another two weeks during which Vicky became more hyper and started to have grandiose thoughts. Scott asked if he could accompany her to her next session and she agreed. With her husband and doctor together, Vicky admitted she was getting sick again. She was anxious about getting out of control and asked to have her medication raised again.

No one said anything close to "I told you so" and the question of whether she needed medication for the rest of her life was still on the table. Vicky felt understood and respected by Dr. Kohut and her husband and knew that if she wanted to try to go off the drugs again both would help her.

I haven't seen her in over four years, but I do see Dr. Kohut regularly. As of this writing, he tells me that Vicky tried one more time to go off her medication, but quickly reversed course once the symptoms re-emerged. This last experiment was more worrisome for Dr. Kohut and Scott because she was completely without medication for five months. Nevertheless, she saw her doctor every week to discuss the diary she and her husband were keeping. When the symptoms reemerged, she once again asked for medication. Her partnership with her husband and doctor has kept her in treatment for over four years, except for that short hiatus. Her treatment agreement, that if she wants to go off medication she will do it with the help of her doctor and husband, stands to this day.

Notes:

Part III
To Commit or not to Commit?

Chapter 10

When to Commit

P hil had to commit his daughter, Amy, for the first time when she was a senior in high school. The family was going through a difficult period that included caring for Amy's grandmother, Phil's mother, who suffered from dementia. Amy was active, playing four varsity sports and writing for the school's literary journal. The whole family was feeling the stress of Phil's mother's illness. For this reason, and because Amy seemed fine on the surface, Phil and his wife did not notice that anything was wrong with their daughter.

Then, one night, Amy attempted suicide by cutting her wrists with a razor blade. Phil rushed her to the emergency room. Phil remembers that night as "the very first really serious sign that got everybody's attention that something was wrong."

Before that night, Phil had not seen any signs of what was to come. "I can recall to this day listening to the psychiatrist who evaluated her saying that my daughter was a master of disguise in terms of concealing her feelings, and it took him [the psychiatrist] a while to understand that she had these major emotional storms going on inside, and she could be laughing and telling you something with an air of conviviality and what she was saying wasn't matching at all with what was going on inside."

After that first hospitalization, Phil learned to watch for signs of Amy's illness more closely. He began to identify when the signs were worsening to the point that she would become a serious danger to herself. In the ten years that followed, Phil would commit his daughter another three times.

Earlier, I described how Matt's mother called the police

There is no universal check list you can use to tell you when you should call for help. But there are certain circumstances that always warrant commitment.

when Matt was arguing with her. Matt had become threatening, and she knew from past experience that he was losing control of his behavior. Having survived many episodes of her son's illness, she knew when it was time to call for help. The signs of illness that Matt's mother responded to and that Phil learned to watch for were different. The signs for which you need to learn to watch, may also be unique.

If you are a family member, the first person to contact when you feel that the situation is growing out of control is the therapist or doctor who has been working with your loved one.

There is no universal check list you can use to tell you when you should call for help. But there are certain circumstances that always warrant commitment. When someone is obviously about to hurt himself or someone else, then the imminent danger of harm signals the need to call in outside help. In fact, this is the most common legal standard for committing someone, against their will, to a hospital.

If you are the doctor or therapist, it is almost always good practice to contact the family to share your observations and concerns.

As you begin this process, remember that you are not the first person who has had to commit a loved one. There are many resources available to you to make the process easier. If you're are a family member, the first person to contact when you feel that the situation is spiraling out of control is the therapist or doctor who has been working with your loved one.

If you are a doctor or therapist, it is almost always good practice to contact the family to share your observations and concerns. Hopefully, you have been working as a team up to this point. But even if you haven't, it's never too late to join forces. For many therapists, this advice goes against their training and ethics. What is said in therapy is supposed to stay in the room, with very few exceptions. Although most therapists are not currently trained this way, an exacerbation of a serious mental illness (e.g., psychotic decompensation) is good cause to breach confidentiality so that you can speak with others who care about your patient. If the limits of confidentiality are clear up front ("If you become sick and it affects your good judgement, then I will need to inform your family to get their help"), there is no ethical dilemma.

There are generally three ways to seek a commitment for a loved one. The method that has been described so far is to call the police or go to the emergency room. In addition, many police departments and

1. Go together to an E.R..
2. Call your local crisis team.
3. Call your local police.

psychiatric emergency rooms work in partnership to keep mentally ill people who commit minor offenses (disturbing the peace) out of jail. A common product of this partnership is the "mobile crisis team" (a.k.a. crisis team; mobile acute crisis team; psychiatric crisis unit, etc.). Usually, mobile crisis teams are based in mental health agencies or hospitals. To find out if your community has one, you can call any psychiatric emergency room or your local police department. Another benefit of this type of intervention is that the mental health workers come to your loved one and evaluate him on the spot. If they judge that hospitalization is warranted, they will try to convince your loved one to accompany them to the hospital. If he refuses, they can initiate the commitment process immediately. Because they're trained in recognizing mental illness, they're less apt to misinterpret your loved one's behavior as something other than a sign of illness (e.g., criminal behavior, due to a negative character trait, etc.). They may also be able to communicate more effectively with your loved one compared to the average police officer who has not received the same specialized training. If no mobile crisis team exists, or is unavailable when you call, then contact your local police. Explain that your loved one is mentally ill and in imminent danger of hurting himself or someone else (if applicable).

In addition to the three avenues just described, there are two less immediate methods: the civil commitment hearing and court ordered outpatient treatment.

In addition to the three avenues just described, there are two less immediate methods: the civil commitment hearing and court ordered outpatient treatment. The process and criteria for civil commitment hearings vary from state to state and are described in the following chapters. About 41 states currently have *outpatient* commitment laws. Under such laws, a physician can file a petition asking the court to make sure a seriously mentally ill person stays in treatment when not in hospital. In the appendix, both inpatient and outpatient commitment laws are summarized. Find your State's laws to determine what the criteria and general procedures are for such commitments.

In this chapter, I focus on identifying when the time has come to seek a commitment (inpatient versus outpatient will be determined in large part by the laws you have available to help your loved one get treatment). To succeed, it is imperative that you believe that commitment is not a permanent violation of your loved one's autonomy. In fact, in most cases it is a means by which you can help your loved one regain control of their lives and their self determination.

Whenever you attempt to have a loved one committed, you may feel like you are trying to take control over their life. If you are already struggling with a tenuous or strained relationship, it is only natural to want to avoid the conflict such a move will create. This avoidance and the desire to not be hurtful often lead to procrastination and second thoughts. This is normal but potentially dangerous for all the reasons I discussed in Chapter 4 (Let Sleeping Dogs Lie?). That is why resolving your ambivalence and guilt is usually the first step in any commitment process.

Resolving your ambivalence and guilt

As right as you think your decision is, it's difficult not to feel guilty sometimes and to falter in your resolve. The term "commitment" conjures up images of physical struggle and straightjackets. When we think of a psychiatric ward, the picture of a nurturing and stabilizing environment is generally not the image that comes to mind. Images from the movie *One Flew Over the Cuckoo's Nest* are far more common.

Like most people, Phil initially had a very negative image of institutions. However, when Amy was committed he learned that the in-patient facility near his home was not what he imagined. He and his wife were able to sit and talk with Amy in a comfortable lounge rather than in the harshly-lit, sterile, and empty isolation room that he expected (based on the portrayals of psychiatric wards he saw in the movies). Phil and his wife were able to visit Amy every day and to speak with her on the telephone almost any time they wanted. The reality of the ward quickly allayed Phil's greatest fear when he first committed his daughter. When she was admitted to the hospital he feared that he had just sentenced her to a terrifying, prison-like environment. The truth is that most in-patient treatment facilities are designed to be comfortable and reassuring.

> *Serious mental illness is like any medical illness. If your loved one had diabetes, you would learn everything you could about the illness and what steps to take to control the disease.*

In order to effectively help your loved one, it is necessary to either work through, or temporarily put aside, the fears and doubts that you have about commitment. The most important thing that you need to do is try to objectively separate myth from reality. Learn about the commitment process and what the facilities in your area are like. Many of the consumer-based organizations described in Chapter 14 can help you to learn about what you can expect from your local mental health facilities.

This advice is relevant for some mental health professionals as well. So many times, those of us who work primarily in out-patient settings hesitate to commit patients because of a fear of facilities with which we are not intimately familiar.

Typically, there is more danger in not seeking commitment than in seeking it. When Amy ran away, Phil lost the power to commit her. The numbers of homeless mentally ill are a sad demonstration that all too often we are reluctant or too late to commit loved ones.

Serious mental illness is like any other medical illness. If your loved one had diabetes, you would learn everything you could about the illness and what steps to take to control the disease. You would have emergency medical numbers by the phone and know the closest emergency facility in case anything unexpected happened. If the diabetes flared up and your loved one became confused and disoriented, you would not hesitate to pursue hospitalization, whether your loved one wanted it or not. And I am fairly certain that you would not feel guilty or ambivalent.

Recognize the warning signs.

If you have gone through previous hospitalizations with your loved one, you very likely know the early warning signs. You know when they're acting out of character and the illness has worsened. Whether you are conscious of it or not, you probably know the signs that signal the need for hospitalization. Take a moment to stop and write down the three most worrisome changes in your loved one's thinking, perceptions, and/or actions that you feel warranted hospitalization in the past.

1.＿＿＿＿＿＿＿＿＿＿＿＿＿＿＿＿＿＿＿＿＿
＿＿＿＿＿＿＿＿＿＿＿＿＿＿＿＿＿＿＿＿＿＿＿
＿＿＿＿＿＿＿＿＿＿＿＿＿＿＿＿＿＿＿＿＿＿＿
2.＿＿＿＿＿＿＿＿＿＿＿＿＿＿＿＿＿＿＿＿＿
＿＿＿＿＿＿＿＿＿＿＿＿＿＿＿＿＿＿＿＿＿＿＿
＿＿＿＿＿＿＿＿＿＿＿＿＿＿＿＿＿＿＿＿＿＿＿
3.＿＿＿＿＿＿＿＿＿＿＿＿＿＿＿＿＿＿＿＿＿
＿＿＿＿＿＿＿＿＿＿＿＿＿＿＿＿＿＿＿＿＿＿＿
＿＿＿＿＿＿＿＿＿＿＿＿＿＿＿＿＿＿＿＿＿＿＿

Keep your list in mind and refer to it often. If you are mindful of the early warning signs, you will be less likely to be caught off guard when the illness flares up. Here are some common signs that others have considered serious enough to contemplate commitment:

- Refuses to take medication when the family and therapist know from past experience that deterioration and harm are imminent,
- Verbally or physically abusive,
- Suicidal ideas (e.g., "I wish I was dead," "I should just end it all," etc.),
- Harms self (e.g., cuts body parts, bangs head, drinks soap, eats dirt, etc.),
- Is destructive of property (own or others),
- Stalks others (e.g., incessant phone calls despite complaints, repeated unwanted visits, etc.),
- Homeless, resulting in harm to self (e.g., exposure to extreme weather conditions without appropriate clothing, poor nutrition, neglect of essential health care, etc.),
- Refuses or is unable to speak with anyone,
- Delusions of grandeur (e.g., has superhuman powers, is famous, knows famous people personally, etc.),
- Talks to self excessively
- Speech is unintelligible,
- Delusions of persecution (e.g., being watched by government agents, possessed by the devil, fears loved

ones intend harm, etc.),
* Command hallucinations (e.g., voices that say "you must kill yourself," etc.),
* Significant deterioration in self-care and hygiene,
* Dangerousness due to disorganization (e.g., starts fires unintentionally by dropping lit cigarettes, etc.),
* Inadequate care of dependants (e.g., neglect, isolates the child or elderly person from other family members, etc.),
* Poor judgement (e.g., uncharacteristically sexually provocative and/or promiscuous, stops paying bills, wild spending sprees, gives away all possessions, loses job due to "eccentric" behavior, fails to keep appointments or fails to follow procedures necessary to receive benefits),
* Health is deteriorating (e.g., self starvation, refuses to seek medical help for other serious illnesses, mixes prescribed medications with illicit drugs, etc.).

He understood that I believed I was helping him, even though he didn't agree that he needed help.

These examples may or may not be relevant to your situation. I list them for two reasons: to give you an idea of what others have found to be important signs and to remind you that you are not the only person who has had to make this decision. In Chapter 14 and in the appendix of this book is a list of resources that can put you in touch with people who have had first hand experience dealing with commitments.

When you commit someone to a hospital you may feel that you have created an irreparable breach in trust. But when it's done from a position of love and support, it is almost always perceived as a gift. From my personal experience with my brother, I know that although it took about four hospitalizations, he eventually came to see my interventions into his life (calling the police and his psychiatrists) as an expression of my love for him. He understood that I believed

I was helping him, even though he didn't agree that he needed help. This was a great source of consolation for both of us because it took him several more years to realize that he was ill and in need of treatment (i.e., for us to agree).

Phil had the same experience with his daughter that I had with my brother. Amy is grown now. Her days of involuntary hospitalizations are behind her. Her father now feels more at peace with what he did, especially after a conversation they had together recently. "She told me the thing she hated most was having her volition and free will interfered with and other people in control over her life. But she also said that if she had not been hospitalized when she had, she believes that she would be dead right now. She thanked me for doing it. I didn't realize I still felt guilty, but I did. Because when she thanked me I almost started to cry, the relief was so great. You know, I think that she's probably right about not being alive if she hadn't been forced into treatment. I know that she's right."

Summary

In this chapter, the questions of whether and when to commit were raised. Since you chose to read it, the answer may be that the time to commit is now. If, after using the techniques in this book, your loved one is still refusing treatment, then you have likely begun to seriously consider commitment as an option. If your loved one is seriously ill and not getting treatment, they need help now. If the same person were suffering from a flare-up of some other medical condition like diabetes, or had been in an accident, you would not hesitate to corral them into the car and take them to the hospital against protestations. Sooner or later, when they recognize that what you did was done out of love, they will likely be grateful. When your loved one is refusing treatment and becoming sicker, you should seriously consider taking the only next step to getting them better: commitment. From my personal and professional experience I find that the benefits far outweigh the risks.

Notes:

Chapter 11

How to Do it

A few months after her first commitment, Phil noticed his daughter was becoming more withdrawn from school and her family. Although he wasn't certain, he suspected she had stopped taking her medication. When he asked her about, it she became hostile and defensive. As the weeks passed, Amy seemed to be slipping away again.

Phil thought she needed to go back to the hospital, but Amy adamantly refused. He was hesitant to consider commitment again because he was afraid of how Amy would react and of the effect it would have on her life. Besides these concerns, the truth was that they still had not mended their relationship from the last time that Amy was committed.

Adding to Phil's indecisiveness was the fact that Amy had not tried to hurt herself. Her symptoms were not obviously life threatening, so Phil felt less justified in forcing the issue once again. He decided to wait and see how things worked out.

Growing increasingly worried, Phil and his wife scheduled a family meeting with Amy's therapist "We had this family meeting but the discussion was unpleasant and unproductive. It was very, very uncomfortable for everybody." At this point, Phil was leaning even further away from another commitment.

He watched and waited and Amy ran away. A few weeks later Phil received the call in the middle of the night that he dreaded yet longed for. Amy had been picked up by the police, she was crying hysterically, asking her father for help.

Because Phil did not act on his instinct, the illness

> *Alcohol and drug addictions often accompany serious mental illnesses. For many, turning to these substances is a form of self-medication, a way to feel better. But in the end, they always worsen the mental illness.*

acted for him, taking the decision out of both his and his daughter's hands. By the time he arrived at the police station, Amy had calmed down and with the help of a police officer had called her therapist who in turn called several inpatient psychiatric facilities to find a bed for her. Phil drove his daughter to the hospital that had a bed available, Amy was evaluated and ultimately committed for thirty days for treatment of her mental illness and a drug problem. By this point she also had a substance abuse disorder. Alcohol and drug addictions often accompany serious mental illnesses. For many, turning to these substances is a form of self-medication, a way to feel better. But in the end, they always worsen the mental illness.

Phil describes the time Amy spent in the hospital as a positive experience for him and his wife, "one thing that a commitment does, if you reject everything else about it, is it helps your sanity. You can relax a little because you know that your family member is in a safe place." Phil and his wife would visit Amy everyday that she was in the hospital. They had many more family meetings while Amy was there, but with a new therapist who they felt was more effective.

Although he was well intentioned, Phil made many mistakes that he wished he hadn't. I hesitated to include a discussion of his errors, as I want to be encouraging rather than focus on failures. Much of what Phil did was positive, like contacting Amy's therapist to have a family meeting. But whether I like it or not, mistakes are always instructive.

What Phil should have done

The first mistake Phil made was that he did not try to find a new therapist for his daughter. Although Amy and her parents disagreed on many things, one thing they agreed upon was that the therapist wasn't helping. You can think of therapists as movies. If you see one you don't like, you don't stop going to the movies altogether or see the same one over and over again. You try another. He could have contacted the doctor that had worked with Amy during her last commitment or the social worker. Amy seemed to like these two people and Phil and his wife definitely felt they were a good fit with their daughter.

You should think of therapists as movies. If you see one you don't like, you don't stop going to the movies altogether or see the same one over and over again. You try another.

One of the most important things a family member can do is to stay active and in touch with any care providers. If a loved one stops going to doctor's appointments, it doesn't mean that the doctor is no longer involved or interested. Even her inpatient doctor and social worker would have been more than happy to advise Phil. When he began to worry about Amy, these people should have been among the first that he contacted.

Although he scheduled a family meeting with Amy's therapist he had only spoken to her out-patient psychiatrist once, the week after she came out of the hospital. During that meeting Phil should have asked to stay in contact with her doctor, to share observations, and to solicit advice. Even if Amy were not a minor, he should have asked for this type of access.

Whether you are a family member or a doctor, you can share your observations without violating the doctor patient relationship. As I mentioned earlier, therapists can pave the way for this type of collaboration by clarifying

Whether you are a family member or a doctor, you can share your observations without violating the doctor patient relationship.

the limits of confidentiality up front ("I would like to hear from your family from time to time, to get a feel for how they think you're doing. Also, if you become sick, I may want to talk with them to get their help."). The bottom line is that if the patient knows that certain types of communication will occur between the doctor and family, then confidentiality is not being violated. The rules have to be a little different when you are dealing with serious mental illnesses because judgement and insight can become severely impaired. That is why we all need to talk to one another and work as a team.

When families actively work with the treatment team, they increase the quality of care. It's not something we're proud of, but most doctors and therapists will feel more accountable when a family member is actively involved. Better yet, we become much better at detecting and responding to any worsening of the illness than when we work in isolation.

One final mistake Phil made is worth noting. He did not have the phone number, nor did he even know of the existence, of the local hospital's mobile crisis team. When Amy refused to be evaluated at the hospital, he could have made a single phone call and likely had her evaluated at home.

Finding and using a mobile crisis team

While maintaining contact and working with doctors is the best possible solution, it has to be recognized that this is not always possible. If you are dealing with a loved one who is an adult and has never been committed and refuses to see a doctor, you may find that you have no one to call. If this is the situation, that doesn't mean that you are alone or only have the police as a resource. Most hospitals that have a psychiatric care unit also have a mobile crisis team. This team is usually made up of Master's level psychologists, social workers, or nurses that perform home visits. Like paramedics, they're typically in close contact with a doctor who is stationed in the psychiatric emergency room. Mobile crisis teams are trained to evaluate, refer to outpatient treatment and if necessary, hospitalize. To find if your community has a mobile crisis team, you should contact your local hospital and ask for the psychiatric emergency room. Usually, a psychiatric nurse will answer your call, or if not, the psychiatrist on call.

When you call explain that you are concerned about a loved one and ask what resources are available in your community. The nurse or doctor will be able to tell you about the mobile crisis team and how to contact them. Add this number to your list of doctors and emergency numbers. Sometimes just knowing that it is there can be a relief.

You will also be able to ask about other out-patient services in your community. Even if you haven't reached a crisis point with your loved one, you should feel free to make a call to the psychiatric emergency room or any other local mental health facility. Don't worry about interrupting someone in the middle of an emergency. If you have, they will let you know and ask you to call back. I recall that during my time covering the psychiatric emergency room when I was in training, I spent as much time fielding such calls as I did evaluating patients in the ER.

The evaluation

After you bring your loved one to the hospital, or call the mobile crisis team, you should immediately ask to speak with the doctor who conducted, or supervised, the evaluation. There are several reasons why it is important for you to speak with the doctor in charge of your loved one's case sooner rather than later. The first is the obvious reason discussed above, you are forming a team with the doctors to insure that your loved one gets the care that they need. There is currently no cure for serious mental illnesses, so it's a good idea to build a network of people familiar with you and your loved one.

Another reason to make sure you talk with the doctor in charge may sound a bit cynical, but it is not. It is realistic. Sometimes doctors working in hospitals don't have the time or resources to give everyone the quality of attention that may be warranted. If you are a mental health professional, it is usually easier to get the doctor's attention. If you are a family member, you may be asked to call back in the morning. In either case, don't let yourself be put off. Act as you would if you were dealing with an accident or a flare-up of some other medical illness like heart disease. In these instances you might feel more comfortable approaching the doctor to find out all the details of the diagnosis, prognosis, and treatment. Find out what is going on and what the plan is. If nothing else is gained, you will at least have let the doctor know that his patient is your loved one and that you hold him accountable for the care that is given.

The doctor who does the diagnosis and intake for your loved one is going to be your biggest ally if your loved one requires a longer stay. An emergency commitment will generally only be for 72 hours. The three-day holding period is all that many states allow without some kind of civil court hearing. The admitting doctor is experienced in the commitment procedure for your state. The length of stay ordered will depend, in large part, on the recommendations of the doctors caring for your loved one.

Calling the police

The idea of having to call the police for help with a loved one seems very dramatic and somehow wrong. We usually call the police when a crime has been committed. However, you may need to call the police when your loved one is out of control because they're trained to act in situations where someone is not in control of their behavior.

If you had a five-year-old child who ran into the street, you would pick him up and restrain him. If he had a temper tantrum and threatened to harm you, you would send him to his room.

Not all police departments offer training in dealing with mental illness, but some do. If your local police department does not offer such training, contact the Memphis Tennessee police department to learn of their crisis intervention program. This program was recognized at a White House conference in 1999 as a model

system for 'decriminalizing' the mentally ill. Ask for literature and pass it along to your local police. I was fortunate in
that the Tucson police had received such specialized training
when I called them about my brother in the early 1980's.
Nevertheless, whenever I called the police to ask for their
help in getting my brother to the hospital, my mother would
become angry with me. She felt protective of my brother, and
as if involving the police was somehow criminalizing him.

One explanation I gave her and have since given to
many family members and mental health professionals is as
follows. If you had a five-year-old child who ran into the
street, you would pick him up and restrain him. If he had a
temper tantrum and threatened to harm you, you would likely send him to his room. When someone is a full grown
adult, you can't physically do any of these things. But the
police can. In my experience, police officers usually restrain
and transport people with mental illness with respect and
dignity. If you feel that your local police force has not
received the proper training to elevate their understanding
and sensitivity to persons with serious mental illness, then
contact your police chief, sheriff, or police commissioner
and suggest that they learn about model used by the
Memphis police department. Better yet, write to the
Memphis police and request literature on their officer training program and mail it directly with a letter to you local
police.

In dealing with Amy's
illness, Phil found the police
to be an invaluable resource.
He said that, "When she was
an adult and her boyfriend
would call us because she
was out of control, I some-

> *More often than not, in my
> experience, police officers
> restrain and transport peo-
> ple with mental illness with
> respect and dignity.*

times actually did go over and physically get involved. But I
wasn't effective and it made things worse between us. As she
became sicker, I realized I couldn't handle her anymore and
neither could her boyfriend. So I would just say, 'call the
police, tell them that she is seriously mentally ill and that she

is suicidal and let them deal with it.' And in every case they have dealt with it and found a way to get her into some kind of treatment."

For Phil, using the police to help with Amy became a safety net, he knew that whenever she got out of control, he could call the police and they would come and bring Amy to the hospital. However, in order for Phil to be able to call the police, he had to accept the fact that when he did there was going to be a scene, "every time I was there it used to break my heart. She would always give the police a hard time. I've seen how she gets really sharp tongued. I mean I'm embarrassed for her when she says some of the things that she says." In Amy's case, she was always in such an excited state when the police arrived that there was no question that she needed help. This scenario is not always the case, sometimes the police come and are not able to help because everything looks fairly normal and calm.

I used to work on a mobile crisis team and we would call this sudden calmness the "ambulance cure." We coined the phrase after evaluating a man with schizophrenia who had been screaming threats at the top of his lungs in a 24 hour convenience store. He accused the clerks of spying on him and demanded that they stop. He was delusional and hearing voices that he told us about when we arrived. After conferring with the psychiatrist at the hospital on our radios, we all agreed that he should be brought in for a 72 hour observation period. By the time the ambulance arrived to transport him to the hospital, he was visibly calmer. By the time the ride was over and he was being evaluated by the ER psychiatrist, he was denying that any of it had happened. He knew that if he talked about the voices or his paranoid fears that the doctor would admit him to the hospital. And since he didn't think he was ill and didn't want to stay, he avoided any topics that would get him admitted. Fortunately, the psychiatrists we worked with trusted our judgement and did not make rash decisions. After three hours in the ER, he began to get agitated again. He started mumbling to his voices and voiced his concern that the clerks had bugged the interview room.

If everything has calmed down by the time the police come, be sure to tell them everything that happened in detail. If threats were made, don't be shy about talking about them. If furniture was turned over and dishes broken, don't straighten up prior to their arrival. Be certain to tell them that they're dealing with someone with a history of serious mental illness and that you are very concerned for their safety. Ask them to bring your loved one to the hospital if they don't offer to do so. If they refuse, ask to speak with their supervisor.

Below are some tips to help you when you call the police:

• Remember police officers are trained to deal with someone who is mentally ill.

• Make sure that when you call the police you specifically tell the dispatcher that the situation they're responding to involves someone who is mentally ill so that the police are aware of what they're walking into.

• If possible, meet the police at the door and describe where your loved one is, why you are concerned and if possible what kind of behavior the police will encounter when they enter.

• Be sure to tell them whether or not your loved one has access to any type of weapon. If there is no weapon, the officers will be less anxious and can focus first on the safety of your loved one. If there is a weapon, they need to know.

• If your loved one has thrown or broken anything, don't try to pick up before the police come. Whatever damage your loved one may have caused may be the only overt sign of illness that the officers can see.

Finally, if you need to call the police to help you with your loved one, please don't blame yourself for doing something awful or inappropriate. The police regularly respond to situations involving people who are seriously mentally ill. Also, remember that you are not alone. The appendix lists resources for families who are dealing with mental illness and many of the web sites offer personal accounts of how other people have handled the same and similar situations.

Chapter 12

Dealing with Betrayal

Even if you believe seeking a commitment is the best thing for your loved one, it doesn't mean you won't suffer some emotional fallout. You know that your loved one is sick and you know that forcing him to take medication is the only chance he will have to ever get better. All that remains is to try again to build an alliance and treatment agreement. But he is likely to feel betrayed by what you have done and not be very open to talking with you about anything. Worse yet, you may feel that he is right. If either of you believe that you have in fact betrayed your loved one's trust, then there can be no partnership or treatment agreement. This is why dealing with feelings of betrayal early on is so vital.

During the initial days your loved one is in the hospital, it is only natural that they will be angry with you. And because they're sicker than usual, it may not be possible for you to have a meaningful conversation. This doesn't mean that you should avoid going to the hospital to visit. Sometimes well meaning hospital staff may even encourage you to wait if they feel you will be upset seeing your loved one so ill. Other times, your loved one may refuse to see you. But it is nevertheless imperative that you visit as often as you can without overburdening yourself. The reason for this is that many people who are forced into the hospital feel their families want to get rid of them and have abandoned them. It's harder for them to believe this if you try to visit the hospital everyday even if it is only for five minutes to say, "Hi, I love you."

At the same time, you need to remember to take care of yourself during this period. If the trips to the hospital are

Acknowledge feelings of betrayal while pointing out that you were being loyal to your conscience.

draining and too overwhelming, only go for the few minutes it takes for your loved one to see that you are there and haven't abandoned them. Then go home and try to relax, watch a movie, go out to dinner with a close friend, take care of yourself. Letting your mind endlessly roll over what is going on in the hospital will not help anyone and can be detrimental to you and your relationship with your loved one. If you are not seeing a therapist of your own, this may be a good opportunity for you to find someone that you can talk to about your situation. Family organizations are particularly helpful in this regard.

At some point during or after the hospitalization, you will need to begin to look for an opportunity to sit down together and have a talk about why you felt you had to have them committed. There is no perfect script for what you should say to your loved one, other than making certain that you are speaking from your heart. It may be a simple as saying: "I had to call the police, I couldn't live with myself if I didn't." Or, "I know you feel angry and betrayed, but I would have felt guilty and that I had let you down if I didn't get you into the hospital."

Turning betrayal into loyalty

A conversation aimed at dealing with feelings of betrayal should always start with an apology and statement that you understand how your loved one feels, " I know you don't feel you need this, I know you are angry with me, I'm very sorry that what I've done is so hurtful to you, but I would like to tell you why I felt like I had to do it." In a large part, this conversation is more of an apology than a justification and you need to be careful not to become

I am not recommending that you apologize for what you did, but rather, for how it made your loved one feel.

accusatory or defensive in any way; acknowledge feelings of betrayal while pointing out that you were being loyal to your conscience.

You may balk at the notion of apologizing. You were acting with your loved one's best interest in mind so you have nothing to be sorry for. I agree. I am not recommending that you apologize for what you did, but rather, for how it made your loved one feel. Here are some general Do's and Don'ts to help you to have a conversation that will aid in mending the relationship.

Do
1. Acknowledge the feelings of betrayal.
2. Ask for forgiveness.
3. Explain why you felt you had to do what you did.
4. Be honest that you would do it again.

Don't
1. Deny the feelings of betrayal.
2. Expect to be forgiven right away.
3. Blame your loved one for what you felt you had to do.
4. Be misleading about what you would do in the future.

There are four main points that you should try to convey to your loved one: your regret, your fear that they will be angry with you and not understand your perspective, why you felt you had to take the actions that you did, and an appeal for their forgiveness.

1. Regret
It is very natural that you may feel regret about "locking-up" your loved one. It's not unlike the regret we feel whenever we impose a restriction on a child (e.g., when you tell a child "go to your room"). Even though it was done with the best intentions doesn't mean that it was

You feel sorry that your conscience led you to do something you know your loved one felt was hurtful.

easy to do and that you are not sorry that you felt you had to do it.

When you have the conversation with your loved one, let them know that you regret having to commit them and wished you didn't feel you had to. Don't blame your loved one for putting you in the position of doing something you'd rather not do, this will only lead to estrangement, not an alliance. Instead, simply state your feelings. You feel sorry that your conscience led you to do something you know your loved one felt was hurtful. In the space below, write down any feelings of regret you have about the commitment and how you might say this to your loved one.

_____

_____

_____

_____

_____

_____

Don't speak in absolute truths like "I had to do this, I had no other choice." Instead say "I felt I had to do this, I felt I had no other choice."

Did you write something that you will be able to convey to your loved one in a way that helps them to understand the dilemma you were in? Put yourself in the shoes of your loved one for a moment and read what you wrote. Is it something that you would respond well to? Would you feel blamed? Or, do you feel like you understand how the person who committed you felt about doing it?

Don't speak in absolute truths like, "I had to do this, I had no other choice." Instead say, "I felt I had to do this, I felt I had no other choice." Emphasize that your values and love led you to do what you did, not that you were "right" to do it.

2. Fear

Explain what it is you were afraid would happen if you didn't have them committed. Preface your fears by acknowledging that your loved one did not fear the same. As you explain the

Also explain that your fears grew out of how deeply you care about them and not from expecting them to behave badly.

fears that you had, it is important that you phrase them in such a way that you are not making accusations about anticipated behavior. Also explain that your fears grew out of how deeply you care about them and not from expecting them to behave badly. Keeping in mind what was said above, write down a few of the fears that you think sharing with your loved one would help to mend the relationship and help them to understand your motivations.

_____

_____

_____

_____

_____

Have a look at what you wrote and refer to the do's and don'ts given above. Did you follow the advice I gave?

3. Actions

Explain why you took the actions that you did. Remind your loved one of the event that precipitated your calling the police or bringing them to the hospital. As you

Don't ask them to agree, only to understand and for-give you for following your conscience.

write down the reason for your actions and the incident, keep in mind that you don't want to sound accusing or angry. This is a conversation in which you are trying to convey your reasoning behind having them committed. Don't ask them to agree, only to understand and forgive you for following your conscience. In the space provided, write down the reasons you pursued a commitment.

_____

_____

_____

_____

_____

_____

4. Appeal for forgiveness and understanding

What you are asking your loved one to do is to try to comprehend why you did what you had to do, how much you love them, and how much their forgiveness means to you. Don't be afraid to let them have the upper hand. In other words, stand firmly on your convictions and don't defend yourself or your decision. You are asking them to forgive you that is all. Listen carefully to what they have to say and see where the dialogue leads.

Don't expect to be successful after only one conversation. It will take several discussions before your loved one's misconceptions about how you feel and why you did what you did can be corrected. If your loved one refuses to talk with you about the commitment, then write it all down in a letter. In fact, even if you have had successful discussions, it's useful to write a letter that covers the four points discussed above. Serious mental illness sometimes makes it difficult to remember. Having your explanation and appeal for forgiveness in writing will help your loved one remember what you said.

I wish I could end this chapter by saying that if you follow the above steps you will have turned your loved one's feelings of betrayal into an understanding and empathy for your predicament. But that would be unrealistic. Whether your loved one is able to forgive, let go of feeling betrayed, and understand your point of view will rely in large part on their innate capacity to accomplish these things. However, I can promise that if you follow the advice given here, you will feel better about what you have done and lessen the conflict in your relationship with your loved one.

_____

_____

_____

_____

_____

_____

Notes:

Part IV
When the Dust Settles

Chapter 13

Keeping them on
Your Team and in Treatment

Whether you successfully arrived at a treatment agreement or safely navigated a commitment, the final step is to not lose any ground and to build on what you have accomplished. If a treatment agreement was made, then your goal is to stay on the same team as your loved one. Don't revert to the old-fashioned approach of "doctor knows best" or worse, "father knows best." Even if you feel you do, it won't matter one iota if you make a point of saying so. Your main goal should be to maintain the collaborative dialogue you have begun.

> *Don't revert to the old-fash-ioned approach of "doctor knows best" or worse, "father knows best."*

When the dust has settled after a commitment, your task is to not lose the ground you have gained and to set the foundation for a more collaborative approach for the future. Work closely with the doctor in charge of your loved one's case. Tell the doctor about the history of poor adherence to medication. Ask about intensive case management and "depo" medications[10].

Both have been found to help improve adherence in people who don't think they're ill. You can read more about these interventions on the *www.VidaPress.com* web site.

---

10. These are long lasting injectable antipsychotic medications. Rather than taking pills daily, the person receives an injection one or two times a month.

Anosognosia, or poor insight, is a symptom of the brain disorder that often does not improve with medication.

Remember, don't expect your loved one to gain insight after the symptoms have lessened. Anosognosia, or poor insight, is a symptom of the brain disorder that often does not improve with medication.

Finally, get help for yourself. If you are a member of the team, then you need to be strong, well rested, and motivated. If you do more than you should, you will lose motivation and risk "burn out." Burn out is a term used by mental health professionals to describe the feeling of complete exhaustion that comes from having been immersed in other peoples' problems for too long. Exhausting yourself will only make you less effective and your loved one feel like a burden.

If you're family, you're in a unique position to help your loved one learn how to cope with mental illness. You knew your loved one before the illness struck, giving you a better grasp of the core person that is often eclipsed by symptoms of the disease. When someone who is seriously mentally ill feels that he is seen for who he is, not just for the diagnosis he has been given, he will be open to learning from you. I think my brother would say that I see him for who he is. Henry is a kind, smart, and creative man. I've learned much from him. He taught me how to throw a baseball and how to ski. He taught me so much growing up and brought humor and magic into my life (like the time, when I was five, he convinced me I had just missed Santa Claus flying by our window). I have learned about compassion, patience and perseverance from him. I take great pleasure in knowing that he has learned a few things from me.

Chapter 14
Resources You Should Know About

This chapter is divided into two sections. The first is a list of family and professional organizations that can provide information and services that you may need. The second part of this chapter is a summary of State commitment laws (both inpatient and outpatient). My hope is that you will use this chapter to obtain information, guidance, and support. Anna-Lisa speaks about how when her mother died she didn't even know that these groups existed and regrets not having become involved earlier. These organizations are invaluable if for no other reason than to reiterate that you are not alone and that you are not the only family experiencing this illness and its traumatic effects.

Many advances are being made in our knowledge about the brain and serious mental illness. By becoming part of the community of people who care most about this information you will not only benefit yourself and loved one, but also serve as a catalyst for further progress by joining the ranks of those of us that are advocates for people with serious mental illness. I invite you to join the relevant organizations listed below, become familiar with your State's mental health laws and lobby for changes as you see fit.

I also urge you to visit the publisher of this book on the World Wide Web. At *www.VidaPress.com* you can subscribe to a newsletter where you will get up-to-date information about advances in treatment of serious mental illness, new research, legal news, and other vital updates that you can use.

Organizations

National Alliance for the Mentally Ill (NAMI)
2101 Wilson Blvd., Suite 302, Arlington, VA 22201
Phone: (703) 524-7600 or (800) 950-NAMI (6254)

NAMI is one of the best sources for both support and information about serious mental illness. It was founded in 1979 by families of mentally ill people who were frustrated by the lack of services, treatment, research, and education available for mentally ill people and their relatives. It has become an influential and important advocacy group with local chapters in almost every major city, as well as in many smaller towns. NAMI boasts a membership that is nearing one-half-million people from all corners of the U.S.A.. People who join NAMI or FAMI (the associated Family Alliance for the Mentally Ill) are usually understanding and caring people who have had very similar experiences to your own. Many chapters offer educational programs involving speakers who are involved in cutting edge research and treatment. Some chapters have hotlines you can call during a crisis or just to get information about services in your area. NAMI also has offers excellent books and pamphlets about mental illness.

National Alliance for Research on Schizophrenia and Depression (NARSAD)
60 Cutter Mill Road, Suite 404, Great Neck, NY 11021
Tel: 516-829-0091, 800-829-8292

NARSAD, also a nonprofit organization, was established to raise money for research into affective disorders and schizophrenia. It has been immensely successful in funding promising new scientists and supporting the research of more senior investigators. NARSAD supported scientists have conducted many landmark studies over the past decade. NARSAD raises more money yearly for psychiatric research than any other organization of its kind. Its free newsletter is a wonderful source of up-to-date information on new research.

National Depressive and Manic Depressive Association (NDMDA)

730 North Franklin Street, Suite 501, Chicago, IL 60610

Phone: (800) 82N-DMDA (826-3632)

This organization consists of people with clinical depression and their families who try to educate the public about depression and manic-depression and help others find treatment. The central branch responds to requests for referrals in other areas of the country and can refer you to a local qualified mental health professionals. If you contact them, you should also consider inquiring about their quarterly newsletter which provides up-to-date information and research findings about depression and manic-depression. The newsletter is free with membership in the association.

Depression Awareness, Recognition, and Treatment (D/ART)

National Institute of Mental Health,

5600 Fishers Lane, Room 10-85, Rockville, MD

Phone: (800) 421-4211

This organization can give you good general information about depression, its signs and symptoms, and the latest in treatment options. D/ART publishes some excellent booklets and brochures about depression that you can request.

National Foundation for Depressive Illness (NAFDI)

P.O. Box 2257, New York, NY 10116

Phone: (800) 248-4344

NAFDI is a nonprofit organization that focuses on educating the public about the symptoms of depression and updating professionals on advances in diagnosis and treatment. They can also send you some clear and concise brochures and pamphlets about depression, as well as refer you to mental health professionals in your area.

Lithium Information Center
8000 Excelsior Drive, Suite 302, Madison, WI 53717
Phone: (608) 836-8070
    This center is part of the Department of Psychiatry at
the University of Wisconsin. It is a well known resource for
information about the use of lithium in the treatment of
bipolar disorder (or manic depression).

American Association of Suicidology
2459 South Ash, Denver, CO 80222
Phone: (303) 692-0985
    This organization offers a variety of printed suicide
prevention materials, primarily for use in schools and other
institutional settings. However, they can also refer you to
suicide hotlines and support groups in your area.

American Psychological Association
750 1st Street, N.E., Washington, D.C. 20002
Phone: (202) 336-5500

American Psychiatric Association
1400 K Street, N.W., Washington, D.C. 20005
Phone: (202) 682-6066

    These last two organizations are the national associa-
tions of the professions of psychology and psychiatry,
respectively. If you contact them, they can send you information about serious mental illnesses and their treatment, as
well as refer you their qualified members in your area. The
American Psychological Association also publishes fact
sheets (*Facts About Manic Depression*, *Facts About
Schizophrenia*, etc.) that are very informative.

Other Resources

Support organizations are another important resource. In most communities, there are support groups for people suffering from mental illness, as well as for their families and loved ones. Contact your local NAMI office for information about local support groups or look in your local newspaper or community newsletter for announcements of meetings.

All of the organizations listed above have excellent web sites that provide important information about the causes of serious mental illness, warning signs to look for, and treatments. Another excellent web site I recommend is *www.Schizophrenia.com.*

Notes:

Literature cited

Amador XF, Flaum M, Andreasen NC, Strauss DH, Yale SA, Clark SC, & Gorman JM. Awareness of illness in schizophrenia and schizoaffective and mood disorders. *Archives of General Psychiatry*, 51:826-836. 1994.

Amador XF & Gorman JM. "Psychopathologic domains and insight in schizophrenia." *Psychiatric Clinics of North America,* 20:27-42, 1998.

Amador XF, "Closing the Gap between Science and Practice," *Civil Rights Law Journal*, in press.

Amador XF, Strauss DH, Yale SA, Flaum M, Endicott J, & Gorman JM. Assessment of Insight in Psychosis. *American Journal of Psychiatry,* 150:873-879. 1993.

Amador XF, Barr W.B.; Economou, A.; Mallin, E.; Marcinko, L.; Yale, S. "Awareness deficits in neurological disorders and schizophrenia." *Schizophrenia Research*, 24(1-2): 96-97, 1997.

Amador XF, Harkavy Friedman J, Kasapis C, Yale SA, Flaum M, & Gorman JM. "Suicidal behavior and its relationship to awareness of illness." *American Journal of Psychiatry,* 153:1185-1188, 1996.

Amador XF & Seckinger RA. "The assessment of insight." *Psychiatric Annals,* 27(12):798-805, 1997.

Amador XF & Strauss DH. Poor insight in schizophrenia. *Psychiatric Quarterly*, 64:305-318. 1993.

Amador XF; Strauss DH; Yale SA & Gorman JM. Awareness of Illness in Schizophrenia. *Schizophrenia Bulletin*, 17:113-132, 1991.

Bartko G., Herczog I. & Zador G. Clinical symptomatology and drug compliance in schizophrenic patients. *Acta Psychiatrica Scandinavica,* 77:74-76. 1988.

McEvoy JP, Applebaum PS, Geller JL, Freter S. Why must some schizophrenic patients be involuntarily committed? The role of insight. *Comprehensive Psychiatry*, 30:13-17. 1989.

Bartko G; Herczog I & Zador G. Clinical Symptomatology and Drug Compliance in Schizophrenic Patients. *Acta Psychiatrica Scandinavica*, 77:74-76, 1988.

Caracci G; Mukherjee S; Roth S & Decina P. Subjective Awareness of Abnormal Involuntary Movements in Chronic Schizophrenic Patients. *American Journal of Psychiatry*, 147:295-298. 1990.

Cuesta MJ & Peralta V. Lack of Insight in Schizophrenia. *Schizophrenia Bulletin*, 20:359-366. 1994.

Flashman LA, McAllister TW, Saykin AJ, Johnson SC, Rick JH, Green RL, Neuroanatomical Correlates of Unawareness of Illness in Schizophrenia. From the Neuropsychology & Brain Imaging Laboratories, Dept. of Psychiatry, Dartmouth Medical School, Lebanon, NH & New Hampshire Hospital, Concord, NH 03301. Presented at the *Biennial Meeting of the International Congress on Schizophrenia Research*, Santa Fe, New Mexico, April 20, 1999

Ghaemi NS & Pope HG, Jr. Lack of Insight in Psychotic and Affective Disorders : A Review of Empirical Studies. *Harvard Review of Psychiatry*, May/June: 22-33. 1994.

Greenfield D; Strauss JS; Bowers MB & Mandelkern M. Insight and Interpretation of Illness in Recovery from Psychosis. *Schizophrenia Bulletin*, 15:245-252. 1989.

Heinrichs DW; Cohen BP & Carpenter WT, Jr. Early Insight and the Management of Schizophrenic Decompensation. *Journal of Nervous and Mental Disease*, 173:133-138. 1985.

Kampman O. Lehtinen K. Compliance in psychoses. *Acta Psychiatrica Scandinavica.* 100(3):167-75, 1999

Lysaker PH; Bell MD; Milstein R; Bryson G & Beam Goulet J. Insight and Psychosocial Treatment Compliance in Schizophrenia. *Psychiatry,* Vol. 57. 1994.

Lysaker PH. Bell MD. Bryson G. Kaplan E. Neurocognitive function and insight in schizophrenia: support for an association with impairments in executive function but not with impairments in global function. *Acta Psychiatrica Scandinavica.* 97(4):297-301, 1998

McEvoy JP; Appelbaum PS; Geller JL & Freter S. Why Must Some Schizophrenic Patients be Involuntarily Committed ? The Role of Insight. *Comprehensive Psychiatry* 30:13-17. 1989.

McEvoy JP, Apperson LJ, Applebaum PS, Ortlip P, Brecosky J, Hammill K. Insight in schizophrenia. Its relationship to acute psychopathology. *Journal of Nervous and Mental Disorders,* 177:43-47. 1989.

McGlashan TH; Levy ST & Carpenter WT, Jr. Integration and Sealing Over: Clinically Distinct Recovery Styles from Schizophrenia. *Archives of General Psychiatry*, 32:1269-1272, 1975.

McGlashan TH & Carpenter WT Jr.. Does attitude toward psychosis relate to outcome? *American Journal of Psychiatry*, 138:797-801. 1981.

Michalakeas A; Skoutas C; Charalambous A; Peristeris A; Marinos V; Keramari E & Theologou A. Insight in Schizophrenia and Mood Disorders and its Relation to Psychopathology. *Acta Psychiatrica Scandinavica*, 90:46-49, 1994.

Mohamed S. Fleming S. Penn DL. Spaulding W. Insight in schizophrenia: its relationship to measures of executive functions. *Journal of Nervous & Mental Disease.* 187(9):525-31, 1999

Morgan KD, Vearnals S, Hutchinson G, Orr KGD, Greenwood K, Sharpley R, Mallet R, Morris R, David A, Leff J, Murray RM. Insight, ethnicity, and neuropsychology in first-onset psychosis. *Schizophrenia Research*, 36(1-3): 144. 1999.

Morgan KD, Orr KGD, Hutchinson G, Vearnals S, Greenwood K, Sharpley M, Mallet R, Morris R, David A, Lefef J, Murray RM. Insight and neuropsychology in first-onset schizophrenia and other psychoses. *Schizophrenia Research*, 36(1-3): 145. 1999.

Smith TE. Hull JW. Santos L. The relationship between symptoms and insight in schizophrenia: a longitudinal per-spective. *Schizophrenia Research.* 33(1-2):63-7, 1998.

Swanson Cl, Jr.; Freudenreich O; McEvoy JP; Nelson L; Kamaraju L & Wilson WH. Insight in Schizophrenia and Mania. *The Journal of Nervous and Mental Disease*, 183:752-755, 1995.

Takai A, Uematsu M, Ueki H, Sone K and Kaiya Hisanobu. Insight and its Related Factors in Chronic Schizophrenic Patients: A preliminary Study. *European Journal of Psychiatry*, 6:159-170, 1992.

Voruganti LN. Heslegrave RJ. Awad AG. Neurocognitive correlates of positive and negative syndromes in schizophrenia. *Canadian Journal of Psychiatry.* 42(10):1066-71, 1997.

Wciorka J. A Clinical Typology of Schizophrenic Patients Attitudes towards their Illness. *Psychopathology*, 21:259-266, 1988.

Wilson WH, Ban T & Guy W.. Flexible System Criteria in Chronic Schizophrenia. *Comprehensive Psychiatry,* 27:259-265. 1986.

World Health Organization. Report of the International Pilot Study of Schizophrenia. Geneva: World Health Organization Press. 1973.

Young DA, Davila R, Scher H.. Unawareness of illness and neuropsychological performance in chronic schizophrenia. *Schizophrenia Research*, 10:117-124. 1993.

Young DA, Zakzanis KK, Baily C, Davila R, Griese J, Sartory G & Thom A. Further Parameters of Insight and Neuropsychological Deficit in Schizophrenia and Other Chronic Mental Disease. *Journal of Nervous and Mental Disease,* 186: 44-50. 1998.

Recommended Readings

Mental Disorders Updates & News
A quarterly newsletter called *Mental Disorders Updates and News* provides a summary of recent research on treatment of serious mental disorders, news about changes in mental health laws, and advances made in our understanding of the causes of mental illness. To receive *M.D. Updates & News* visit the Vida Press website at *www.VidaPress.com* or write to Vida Press, M.D. Updates & News, 1150 Smith Road, Peconic New York, 11958.

NAMI Newsletter
The NAMI newsletter is an excellent source of information on research, legal and political issues pertaining to the seriously mentally ill, and general information that you can use. Contact NAMI by writing to them at: 2101 Wilson Blvd., Suite 302, Arlington, VA 2220; or call (703) 524-7600, or (800) 950-NAMI (6254).

Surviving Schizophrenia: A manual for Families Consumers and Providers .(Third Edition)
E. Fuller Torrey, Harper perennial Library, 2000.

Understanding Schizophrenia
RSE Keefe and P Harvey, The Free Press, Simon & Schuster, 1994.

When Someone You Love is Depressed: How to help your loved one without losing yourself.
L Rosen and XF Amador, The Free Press, Simon & Schuster, 1996. Paperback: Fireside, Simon & Schuster, 1997.

Insight and Psychosis
Amador XF & David A, Editors, Oxford University Press, 1997

Appendix

Attitudes and Beliefs Checklist (ABC)

This checklist is literally as important to reaching a treatment agreement as learning your ABC's was to reading and writing. To complete the ABC you need not ask the suggested questions. Sometimes you will get the information needed by simply listening for it.

Medication
What do you think about psychiatric medications?
Do you think that someone who takes a psychiatric drug is weak?
What do you like about the medication you've been prescribed?
What don't you like about it?
How does it make you feel about yourself when you take the pills?
Do you think you need to take medication?
How long do you think you'll need to take medication?

Mental Illness
What do you think of people who are mentally ill?
What do you think causes mental illness?
Do you have any mental illness?
Would having a mental illness make you feel like a failure?
How is mental illness different from other illnesses?
Why do you think others say you have a mental illness?
Is your mental illness permanent or temporary?

Frustrations
How do you feel about being in the hospital?
Does it bother you not to work?
Does it bother you that you don't have a "boyfriend/girlfriend?"
How do you feel about the fact that some people want you

to take psychiatric drugs?
How do you feel about not reaching the goals you set for
yourself?

Self Concept and Desires
What do you most want to accomplish in life?
What are your goals for the next month (year, five years,
etc.)?
What kind of job, if any, can you work at right now?
Do you feel like a success or failure?

Summary of U.S. Commitment Laws by State

When you read the summary of the laws for your
state it is important to keep in mind that these laws are the
standards that a judge in a civil commitment proceeding
uses to determine whether or not to order a commitment
(a.k.a. assisted treatment). Most likely, you will use one of
the other methods described in Chapter 12 and the hospital
or treatment team will work through the official aspects of
seeking a commitment. It is still a very useful to learn what
your state considers to be the criteria for commitment and
to ask yourself if you think the law is really fair.

The Treatment Advocacy Center compiled the information in this section, which is periodically updated on the
Center's website *www.psychlaws.org.* For the most current
information about your state's commitment law, you should
consult your local library or an attorney in your state. The
Center is a non-profit organization working to reform the
legal systems that prevent individuals who are most in need
of assisted treatment from getting it. The Center is a
resource for individuals seeking to reform assisted treatment laws in their own states. Although the Center does not
represent individuals, the attorneys at the Center can assist
families seeking treatment for their loved ones by explaining state laws governing assisted treatment decisions and
providing guidance about the process of obtaining assisted
treatment. The Center also serves as a clearinghouse for

information about assisted treatment, the consequences of non-treatment and current developments in assisted treatment law. The Center can be reached through its website or by calling 703-294-6001.

ALABAMA
ALA. CODE § 22-52-10.4
ALA. CODE § 22-52-10.2
Inpatient: A real and present danger to self/others, without treatment will continue to suffer mental distress and deterioration of ability to function independently, and unable to make a rational and informed decision concerning treatment.

Outpatient: Without treatment will continue to suffer mental distress and deterioration of the ability to function independently and the respondent is unable to make a rational and informed decision concerning treatment.

ALASKA
ALASKA STAT. § 47.30.755(a)
ALASKA STAT. § 47.30.915(7)
Inpatient and Outpatient: (1) Danger to self/others; (2) in danger from inability to provide basic needs for food, clothing, shelter, or personal safety; or (3) without treatment will suffer severe and abnormal mental, emotional, or physical distress associated with significant cognitive impairment.

ARIZONA
ARIZ. REV. STAT. § 36-540(A)
ARIZ. REV. STAT. § 36-501(4)
ARIZ. REV. STAT. § 36-501(5)
ARIZ. REV. STAT. § 36-501(15)
ARIZ. REV. STAT. § 36-501(29)
Inpatient and Outpatient: (1) Danger to self/others; (2) in danger from inability to provide basic physical needs; or (3) likely to suffer severe and abnormal mental emotional

or physical harm without treatment, likely to benefit from treatment, and substantially impaired capacity to make informed decisions regarding treatment.

ARKANSAS
ARK. CODE ANN. § 20-47-207(c)

Inpatient and Outpatient: Clear and present danger to self/others.

CALIFORNIA
CALIF. WELF. & INST. CODE § 5250
CALIF. WELF. & INST. CODE § 5008(h)(1)

Inpatient and Outpatient: (1) Danger to self/others or (2) unable to provide for basic personal needs for food, clothing, or shelter.

COLORADO
COLO. REV. STAT. § 27-10-107
COLO. REV. STAT. § 27-10-102(5)

Inpatient and Outpatient: (1) Danger to self/others; (2) in danger of serious physical harm due to inability to provide essential human needs of food, clothing, shelter, and medical care; (3) cannot manage resources or conduct social relations so that health or safety is significantly endangered and lacks capacity to understand this is so; or (4) criteria allowing for those in need of care of because of pending loss of support of a relative who is a caregiver.

CONNECTICUT
CONN. GEN. STAT. ANN. § 17a-498(c)
CONN. GEN. STAT. ANN. § Sec. 17a-495(a)

Inpatient: (1) Danger to self/others or (2) in danger of serious harm from inability to provide for basic needs such as essential food, clothing, shelter or safety and unable to make a rational and informed decision concerning treatment.

DELAWARE
DEL. CODE ANN. tit. 16, § 5001(1)

Inpatient and Outpatient: Real and present danger to self/others/property, in need of treatment, and unable to make responsible decisions with respect to hospitalization.

DISTRICT OF COLUMBIA
CODE ANN. § 21-545(b)

Inpatient and Outpatient: Danger to self/others.

FLORIDA
FLA. STAT. ANN. § 394.467(1)

Inpatient: Unable or refuses to make responsible decisions with respect to voluntary placement for treatment AND either (1) without treatment, incapable of surviving alone or with the help of willing family or friends, and likely to suffer from neglect or refuse to care for himself/herself, will pose a real and present threat of substantial harm to well-being OR (2) danger to self/others, as evidenced by recent behavior.

GEORGIA
GA. CODE ANN. § 37-3-1(9.1)
GA. CODE ANN. § 37-3-1(12.1)

Inpatient. In need of involuntary treatment AND (1) imminent danger to self/others, evidenced by recent overt acts or expressed threats of violence OR (2) unable to care for physical health and safety so as to create an imminently life-endangering crisis and in need of involuntary treatment.

Outpatient: Based on treatment history or current mental status, requires outpatient treatment in order to avoid predictably and imminently becoming an inpatient and unable to voluntarily seek or comply with outpatient treatment.

HAWAII
HAW. REV. STAT. § 334-60.2
HAW. REV. STAT. § 334-121
HAW. REV. STAT. § 334-1

Inpatient: In need of treatment AND either (1) imminent danger to self/others, including that of substantial emotional injuries to others; OR (2) unable to provide for basic personal needs for food, clothing, or shelter, unable to make or communicate rational decisions concerning personal welfare, and lacking the capacity to understand that this is so; OR (3) behavior and previous history indicate a disabling mental illness and unable to make rational decisions concerning treatment.

Outpatient: Either previous inpatient hospital treatment for a severe mental disorder or substance abuse OR previously been imminently dangerous to self/others OR meets no. 2, above AND capable of surviving safely in the community with available supervision; based on the treatment history and current behavior, treatment is needed to prevent deterioration predictably resulting in imminent danger to self/others; unable to make a rational decisions concerning treatment; and outpatient treatment ordered is likely to be beneficial.

IDAHO
IDAHO CODE § 66-329(k)
IDAHO CODE § 66-317(k), (m)
IDAHO CODE § 66-339A

Inpatient: (1) Danger to self/others or (2) in danger of serious physical harm due to inability to provide for essential needs.

Outpatient: Without treatment likely to become danger to self /others, lacks capacity to make informed treatment decisions, previous psychiatric hospitalization, previously failed to substantially comply with the prescribed course of outpatient treatment, and patient's disorder likely to respond to the treatment.

ILLINOIS
405 ILL. COMP. STAT. 5/1-119
Inpatient and Outpatient: (1) Danger to self/others or
(2) unable to provide for basic physical needs so as to
guard against serious harm.

INDIANIA
IND. CODE ANN. § 12-26-7-5(a)
IND. CODE ANN. § 12-26-14-1
Inpatient: (1) danger to self/others; or in danger of
coming to harm because either (2) unable to provide for
food, clothing, shelter, or other essential human needs OR
(3) substantial impairment or obvious deterioration that
results in inability to function independently.
Outpatient: Same as for inpatient except must also be
likely to benefit from the recommended outpatient treatment program and not be likely to meet inpatient standard
if compliant with the recommended program.

IOWA
IOWA CODE § 229.14
IOWA CODE § 229.1(15)
Inpatient and Outpatient: Lacks sufficient judgment to
make responsible decisions concerning treatment AND is
either (1) a danger to self/others, including that of serious
emotional injuries to family members and others OR (2)
unable to satisfy need for nourishment, clothing, essential
medical care, or shelter so that it is likely that the person
will suffer physical injury, physical debilitation, or death.

KANSAS
KAN. STAT. ANN. § 59-2946a(f)(1)
KAN. STAT. ANN. § 59-2967(a)
Inpatient: Lacks capacity to make informed decision
concerning treatment AND either (1) danger to self/oth-
ers/property OR (2) substantially unable to provide for
basic needs, such as food, clothing, shelter, health or safety.

Outpatient: Same as for inpatient except must also be likely to comply with outpatient treatment order and not likely be danger to self/others/community while subject to outpatient treatment order.

KENTUCKY
KY. REV. STAT. ANN. § 202A.026
KY. REV. STAT. ANN. § 202A.011(2)
Inpatient and Outpatient: Danger to self/others/family, including actions which deprive self/others/family of basic means of survival such as provision for reasonable shelter, food or clothing; can reasonably benefit from treatment; and hospitalization is the least restrictive form of treatment available.

LOUISIANA
LA. REV. STAT. ANN. § 28:55(E)(1)
LA. REV. STAT. ANN. § 28:2(3), (4), (10)
Inpatient and Outpatient: (1) Danger to self/others or (2) unable to provide for basic physical needs, such as essential food, clothing, medical care, and shelter, and unable to survive safely in freedom or guard against serious harm.

MAINE ME. REV. STAT. ANN. tit. 34-B, § 3864(6)(A)
ME. REV. STAT. ANN. tit. 34B, § 3801(4)
Inpatient: Inpatient hospitalization is the best available means for treatment of the patient, the Court is satisfied with the submitted treatment plan AND, based on recent actions or behavior, either (1) danger to self/others OR (2) severe physical or mental impairment or injury likely to result without treatment.

MARYLAND
MD. CODE ANN., HEALTH-GEN. § 10-632(e)(2)
Inpatient: Danger to self/others, in need of treatment, and unable or unwilling to be voluntarily admitted.

MASSACHUSETTS
MASS. GEN. LAWS ANN. ch. 123, § 8(a)
MASS. GEN. LAWS ANN. ch. 123, § 1
Inpatient: (1) Danger to self/others or (2) very substantial risk of physical impairment or injury because unable to protect himself/herself in the community.

MICHIGAN
MICH. COMP. LAWS ANN. § 330.1401
Inpatient and Outpatient: (1) Danger to self others; (2) unable to attend to basic physical needs such as food, clothing, or shelter necessary to avoid serious harm in the near future; or (3) unable to understand need for treatment and continued behavior reasonably expected to result in significant physical harm to self/others.

MINNESOTA
MINN. STAT. ANN. § 253B.09(1)
MINN. STAT. ANN. § 253B.02(13)(a), (17)
Inpatient and Outpatient: (1) A clear danger to others OR the likelihood of physical harm to self/others as demonstrated by either (2) failure to obtain necessary food, clothing, shelter, or medical care OR (3) a recent attempt or threat to harm self/others.

MISSISSIPPI
MISS. CODE ANN. § 41-21-73(4)
MISS. CODE ANN. § 41-21-61(e)
Inpatient and Outpatient: A substantial likelihood of physical harm to self/others as demonstrated by (1) a recent attempt or threat to harm self/others or (2) failure to provide necessary food, clothing, shelter or medical care. Explicitly includes person who, based on treatment history, is in need of treatment to prevent further disability or deterioration predictably resulting in danger to self/others if informed decisions concerning treatment.

MISSOURI
MO. ANN. STAT. § 632.335(4)
MO. ANN. STAT. § 632.005(9)

Inpatient and Outpatient: (1) Danger to self/others and (2) substantial risk that serious physical harm will result due to an impairment in capacity to make treatment decisions, evidenced by inability to provide for basic necessities of food, clothing, shelter, safety, medical care, or necessary mental health care. Evidence may also include past patterns of behavior.

MONTANA
MONT. CODE ANN. § 53-21-126(1)
MONT. CODE ANN. § 53-21-127(2)(d)

Inpatient and Outpatient: In determining whether the respondent requires commitment, the court shall consider the following (1) whether substantially unable to provide for basic needs of food, clothing, shelter, health, or safety; (2) whether recently caused self-injury or injury to others; (3) whether imminent danger to self/others; and (4) whether the respondent's mental disorder, demonstrated by the respondent's recent acts or omissions, will, if untreated, predictably result in deterioration to meet considerations nos. 1, 2 or 3. Predictability may be established by the respondent's relevant medical history. Commitments based solely on consideration no. 4 must be on an outpatient basis.

NEBRASKA
NEB. REV. STAT. § 83-1037
NEB. REV. STAT. § 83-1009

Inpatient and Outpatient: (1) Danger to self/others, as manifested by recent threats/acts of violence or (2) substantial risk of serious harm evidenced by inability to provide for basic human needs, including food, clothing, shelter, essential medical care, or personal safety.

NEVADA
NEV. REV. STAT. § 433A.310(1)
NEV. REV. STAT. § 433A.115
Inpatient: Clear and present danger of harm to self/others and diminished capacity to conduct affairs, social relations, or care for personal needs. Explicitly includes the inability, without assistance, to satisfy need for nourishment, personal/medical care, shelter, self-protection or safety.

NEW HAMPSHIRE
N.H. REV. STAT. ANN. § 135-C:34
N.H. REV. STAT. ANN. § 135-C:27
Inpatient and Outpatient: A potentially serious likelihood of danger to self/others as evidenced by either (1) recent infliction of serious bodily injury, attempted suicide, or serious self-injury in last 40 days which is likely to reoccur without treatment; (2) threatened infliction serious bodily injury on self in last 40 days, and that without treatment an act or attempt of serious self-injury will likely occur; (3) lacks capacity to care for own welfare and a likelihood of death, serious bodily injury, or serious debilitation; (4) severely mentally disabled for at least one year, involuntary admission within last 2 years, refusal of necessary treatment and substantial probability that refusal will lead to death, serious bodily injury, or serious debilitation; OR (5) threatened, attempted or actual act of violence in last 40 days.

NEW JERSEY
N.J. STAT. ANN. § 30:4-27.2(m)
N.J. STAT. ANN. § 30:4-27.2(r)
N.J. STAT. ANN. § 30:4-27.2(h)
N.J. STAT. ANN. § 30:4-27.2(i)
Inpatient: Danger to self/others/property, unwilling to be admitted voluntarily, and in need of treatment. Danger to self explicitly includes the inability, without assistance, to satisfy need for nourishment, essential medical care or shelter.

NEW MEXICO
N.M. STAT. ANN. § 43-1-11(C)
N.M. STAT. ANN. § 43-1-3(M)
N.M. STAT. ANN. § 43-1-3(N)

Inpatient: Danger to self /others, likely to benefit from treatment, and proposed commitment is consistent with treatment needs and least drastic means. Harm to self includes grave passive neglect.

NEW YORK
N.Y. MENTAL HYG. LAW § 9.31(c)
N.Y. MENTAL HYG. LAW § 9.01
N.Y. MENTAL HYG. LAW § 9.60(C)

Inpatient: Danger to self/others, treatment in hospital is essential to welfare, and is unable to understand need for care and treatment.

Outpatient: Unlikely to survive safely in community without supervision, history of noncompliance which includes two hospitalizations in past 36 months or acts/threat/attempt of violence to self/others in 48 months immediately preceding petition filing, unlikely to voluntarily participate, needs in order to prevent relapse or deterioration likely to result in serious harm to self/others, and likely to benefit from assisted treatment.

NORTH CAROLINA
N.C. GEN. STAT. § 122C-268(j)
N.C. GEN. STAT. § 122C-3(11)
N.C. GEN. STAT. § 122C-267(h)
N.C. GEN. STAT. § 122C-263(d)(1)

Inpatient: Danger to self/others/property. Explicitly includes reasonable probability of suffering serious physical debilitation from the inability to, without assistance, either exercise self-control, judgment, and discretion in conduct and social relations; OR satisfy need for nourishment, personal or medical care, shelter, or self-protection and safety.

Outpatient: Capable of surviving safely in community

with available supervision, in need of treatment to prevent further deterioration predictably resulting in dangerousness, and inability to make informed decision to seek/comply with voluntary treatment.
ND N.D. CENT. CODE § 25-03.1-07

NORTH DAKOTA
CENT. CODE § 25-03.1-02(11)
Inpatient and Outpatient: Danger to self/others/property if not treated. Harm to self includes substantial likelihood of deterioration in physical health/substantial injury/disease/death, based upon recent poor self-control or judgment in providing shelter/nutrition/personal care; or substantial deterioration in mental health predictably resulting in danger to self/others/property.

OHIO
OHIO REV. CODE ANN. § 5122.15(C)
OHIO REV. CODE ANN. § 5122.01(B)
Inpatient and Outpatient: (1) Danger to self/others; (2) substantial and immediate risk of serious physical impairment or injury to self as manifested inability to provide for basic physical needs and provision for needs is unavailable in community; or (3) needs and would benefit from treatment as evidenced by behavior creating grave and imminent risk to substantial rights of others/self.

OKLAHOMA
OKLA. STAT. ANN. tit. 43A, § 1-103(14)
Inpatient and outpatient: (1) Danger to self/others evidenced by recent acts/threats; (2) serious harm in near future from inability to attend to basic physical needs such as food, clothing, or shelter; or (3) person appears to require inpatient treatment and treatment is reasonably believed to prevent progressively more debilitating mental impairment.

OREGON
OR. REV. STAT. § 426.005(1)(d)

Inpatient and Outpatient: (1) Danger to self/others; (2) unable to provide for basic personal needs and is not receiving care necessary for health/safety; or (3) chronic mental illness, two hospitalizations in previous three years, symptoms/behavior substantially similar to those that led to the previous hospitalizations, and will continue to physically or mentally deteriorate to either standard (1) or (2) if untreated.

PENNSYLVANIA
50 PA. CONS. STAT. ANN. § 7301(A).

Inpatient and Outpatient: Clear and present danger to self/others; includes inability, without assistance, to satisfy need for nourishment, personal or medical care, shelter, or self-protection and safety, and reasonable probability that death, serious bodily injury or serious physical debilitation would ensue within 30 days.

RHODE ISLAND
R.I. GEN. LAWS § 40.1-5-8(j)
R.I. GEN. LAWS § 40.1-5-2 (7)(i)
R.I. GEN. LAWS § 40.1-5-2 (8)

Inpatient and Outpatient: In need of care/treatment in a facility and, if unsupervised in the community, would be a danger to self/others. Explicitly includes substantial risk of harm manifested by grave, clear and present risk to physical health and safety.

SOUTH CAROLINA
S.C. CODE ANN. § 44-17-580
S.C. CODE ANN. § 44-23-10(2)

Inpatient and Outpatient: Needs treatment and either (1) unable to make responsible decisions with respect to treatment; OR (2) likelihood of serious harm to self/others, including the substantial risk of physical impairment from inability to protect oneself in community and provisions for protection are unavailable.

SOUTH DAKOTA
S.D. CODIFIED LAWS § 27A-1-2
S.D. CODIFIED LAWS § 27A-1-1 (4)
S.D. CODIFIED LAWS § 27A-1-1(5)
Inpatient and Outpatient: Danger to self/others, as evidenced by recent acts, and needs and is likely to benefit from treatment. Danger to self includes danger of serious personal harm in the very near future evidenced by inability to provide for some basic human needs such as food, clothing, shelter, physical health, or personal safety, or arrests for criminal behavior due to mental illness.

TENNESSEE
TENN. CODE ANN. § 33-6-104
Inpatient: In need of care, training, or treatment and likelihood of serious harm, which includes the inability to avoid severe impairment or injury from specific risks.

TEXAS
TEX. HEALTH & SAFETY CODE ANN. § 574.034
TEX. HEALTH & SAFETY CODE ANN. § 574.035
TEX. HEALTH & SAFETY CODE ANN. § 574.034
TEX. HEALTH & SAFETY CODE ANN. § 574.035
Inpatient: (1) Danger to self/others; or (2) severe and abnormal mental, emotional, or physical distress; substantial mental or physical deterioration of ability to function independently, exhibited by the inability to provide for basic needs, including food, clothing, health, or safety; and inability to make rational and informed treatment decisions.

Outpatient: (1) Danger to self/others; or (2) severe and persistent mental illness; if untreated will suffer severe and abnormal mental, emotional, or physical distress; and deterioration of the ability to function independently and inability to live safely in community; and inability to voluntarily and effectively participate in outpatient treatment as demonstrated by actions of past two years or the inability to make an informed treatment decision.

UTAH
UTAH CODE ANN. § 62A-12-234(10).
Inpatient and Outpatient: Inability to make rational treatment decision and immediate danger to self/others, including inability to provide the basic necessities of life such as food, clothing, and shelter.

VERMONT
VT. STAT. ANN. tit. 18, § 7611
VT. STAT. ANN. tit. 18, § 7101(17)
VT. STAT. ANN. tit. 18, § 7101(16)
Inpatient and Outpatient: (1) Danger to self/others. Danger to others includes presenting a danger to persons in his/her care. Danger to self can be the inability, without assistance, to satisfy need for nourishment, personal or medical care, shelter, or self-protection and safety, so that probable death, substantial physical bodily injury, serious mental deterioration or physical debilitation or disease will ensue. (2) A patient who is receiving adequate treatment, and who, if such treatment is discontinued, is likely to deteriorate to the standard in (1).

VIRGINIA
VA.CODE ANN. § 37.1-67.3
VA. CODE ANN. § 37.1-67.3
Inpatient: (1) Imminent danger to self/others; or (2) so seriously mentally ill as to be substantially unable to care for self.
Outpatient: Same as for inpatient plus is competent to understand the stipulations of treatment, wants to live in community and agrees to abide by treatment plan, has capacity to comply with treatment plan, ordered treatment can be delivered on outpatient basis, and can be monitored by community services board or designated providers.

WASHINGTON
WASH. REV. CODE ANN. § 71.05.240
WASH. REV. CODE ANN. § 71.05.240
WASH. REV. CODE ANN. § 71.05.020(14)
WASH. REV. CODE ANN. § 71.05.020(9)
WASH. REV. CODE ANN. § 71.05.020(11)
WASH. REV. CODE ANN. § 71.05.020(26)

Inpatient: (1) Danger to self/others/property; or (2) in danger of serious physical harm from failure to provide for essential human needs of health or safety; or (3) severe deterioration in routine functioning evidenced by loss of cognitive or volitional control and not receiving essential care.

Outpatient: Same as inpatient, if outpatient treatment is in best interest of person.

WEST VIRGINIA
W. VA. CODE § 27-5-4(j)
W. VA. CODE §27-1-12

Inpatient and Outpatient: Danger to self/others, includes active or passive conduct demonstrating danger to self.

WISCONSIN
WIS. STAT. ANN. § 51.20(1)(a)1
WIS. STAT. ANN. § 51.20(1)(a)2
WIS. STAT. ANN. § 51.20(1)(ab)

Inpatient and Outpatient: (1) Danger to self/others as evidenced by recent acts/threats; (2) substantial probability of physical impairment/injury to self as evidenced by recent acts/omissions; (3) inability to satisfy basic needs for nourishment, medical care, shelter or safety so that substantial probability of imminent death, serious physical injury, serious physical debilitation or serious physical disease; or (4) substantial inability to make informed treatment choice, needs care or treatment to prevent deterioration, and substantial probability that if untreated will lack services for health or safety and suffer severe mental, emo-

tional or physical harm that will result in the loss of ability
to function in community or loss of cognitive or volitional
control over thoughts or actions.

WYOMING
WYO. STAT. ANN. § 25-10-110(j)
WYO. STAT. ANN. § 25-10-101(a)(ix)
WYO. STAT. ANN. § 25-10-101(a)(ii)
WYO. STAT. ANN. § 25-10-110(j)(ii)

Inpatient and Outpatient: (1) Danger to self/others; (2)
unable, without available assistance, to satisfy basic needs
for nourishment, essential medical care, shelter or safety so
it is likely that death, serious physical injury, serious physical debilitation, serious mental debilitation, destabilization
from lack of or refusal to take prescribed psychotropic
medications for a diagnosed condition or serious physical
disease will imminently ensue.

Research on Insight

Here, I provide an annotated bibliography of a number of research studies on insight into illness. An overwhelming majority of these studies were conducted over the last five to ten years. Before presenting this research, a brief history about why there has been an explosion of research in recent years is relevant.

History

In 1990, my colleagues at Columbia University and I began a program of research on poor insight in patients with serious mental disorders. But the program almost floundered before it got started when we quickly came up against some methodological obstacles. The most obvious and problematic hurdle we had to cross was that of defining what it was we were talking about when we used the term "insight." As it turns out, although much had been written about "insight," from a psychoanalytic perspective, the authors were frequently talking about apples and oranges and sometimes even bananas. Worse was the fact that most of the literature was theoretical and did not involve any empirical research. This circumstance, and the fact that there was no widely used measure of insight into illness that we could use in our study forced us to take a step back and reevaluate the lay of the land. The result was a paper written for the National Institute of Mental Health's Journal, *Schizophrenia Bulletin*, that focuses on overcoming methodological and conceptual barriers to doing research on insight.

In some ways the conceptual barriers were easier to overcome because by the start of this decade, called the "Decade of the Brain" by the National Institute of Mental Health, there was renewed hope and excitement about uncovering the *neurocognitive* underpinnings of all kinds of mental activity.

For the first time in the history of mankind we have

been able to not only take detailed pictures of brain structure, but also actually take snapshots of how the brain is
functioning. Answers to questions such as what part of the
brain is active when a patient is hallucinating have been
answered. The new technology even allows us to have a
look at which neurotransmitters, the chemical messengers
of the brain, are being used in different parts of the brain
during various mental tasks. What does all this have to do
with insight into illness and treatment refusal? A lot.

By the start of the last decade, the study of consciousness and specific mental activities like "self-awareness"
had become respectable again. Not since the early 1900's
have psychologists and psychiatrists been so willing to
devote scientific careers to studying consciousness. So it
came as no surprise that our goal to stimulate research on
the problem of denial of illness and treatment refusal was
helped by the intellectual climate at the time. But there was
still the problem of overcoming decades of opinion that
poor awareness of illness was just stubbornness or denial.

In our view, there had been a rush to judgement both
by clinicians and family members. Statements such as "I'm
not sick and I don't need help" uttered by someone with
serious mental illness were labeled as defensiveness, as
stemming from denial. But this explanation didn't make
sense to me when encountering people like Matt from
chapter one who thought he was in a psychiatric ward for a
physical check-up and nothing else. What was needed was
a fresh start.

We began by creating guidelines for talking about
insight and for conducting research on the problem.
Conceptually neutral terms like "unawareness of illness"
should be used and new methods for assessing the various
types of unawareness were needed. Drawing from the literature that existed at that time, we developed specific recommendations for dealing with the problems of conducting
meaningful research in this area. Our explicitly stated goal
was to stimulate research in the field. And it worked. In the
ten years prior to the publication of these guidelines only

19 empirical studies on insight in psychotic patients could be found in the published research literature. In only the first five years since, the results of over 70 research studies have been published! Scientists have learned a lot over the past ten years and the time to convey that knowledge to the people who need it most has come.

Below, I provide you with a summary of some of the recent research. Among the research reviewed are studies of brain function/structure and insight, medication adherence and insight, involuntary commitment and insight, and studies of other interventions (video confrontation) aimed at improving insight into illness. If you are interested in staying abreast of further developments visit the publisher's website at *www.VidaPress.com.*

Poor Insight is Common in Schizophrenia and Bipolar Disorder

Recent studies find that about 60% of patients with schizophrenia and bipolar disorder show poor insight into their illness. Early estimates of poor insight in patients with schizophrenia were as high as 81% (W.H.O., International Pilot Study of Schizophrenia) and 89% (Wilson et al, 1986). Although both of these studies were multi-national and involved well over 700 subjects each, they measured insight with a single item from the present state examination (PSE) that required raters to categorize patients as having either "good" or "poor" insight. Most studies conducted over the past ten years use measures of insight that are dimensional and cover a wide range of unawareness phenomena (e.g. awareness of specific symptoms). Of interest is the fact that several studies also find that about 50% of patients with schizophrenia are unaware of their tardive dyskinesia (i.e., they have anosognosia for the specific signs and symptoms of this movement disorder).

Amador XF, Flaum M, Andreasen NC, Strauss DH, Yale SA, Clark SC, & Gorman JM. Awareness of illness in schizophrenia and schizoaffective and mood disorders. *Archives of General Psychiatry*, 51:826-836. 1994.

Ghaemi NS & Pope HG, Jr. Lack of Insight in Psychotic and Affective Disorders : A Review of Empirical Studies. *Harvard Review of Psychiatry*, May/June: 22-33. 1994.

World Health Organization. Report of the International Pilot Study of Schizophrenia. Geneva: World Health Organization Press. 1973.

Wilson WH, Ban T & Guy W.. Flexible System Criteria in Chronic Schizophrenia. *Comprehensive Psychiatry*, 27:259-265. 1986.

Young DA, Zakzanis KK, Baily C, Davila R, Griese J, Sartory G & Thom A.. Further Parameters of Insight and Neuropsychological Deficit in Schizophrenia and Other Chronic Mental Disease. *Journal of Nervous and Mental Disease*, 186: 44-50. 1998.

Kasapis C, Amador XF, Yale SA, Strauss DH, Gorman JM.. Poor insight in schizophrenia: Neuropsychological and defensive aspects. *Schizophrenia Research*, 15:123. 1995.

Morgan KD, Vearnals S, Hutchinson G, Orr KGD, Greenwood K, Sharpley R, Mallet R, Morris R, David A, Leff J, Murray RM.. Insight, ethnicity, and neuropsychology in first-onset psychosis. *Schizophrenia Research*, 36(1-3): 144. 1999.

Morgan KD, Orr KGD, Hutchinson G, Vearnals S, Greenwood K, Sharpley M, Mallet R, Morris R, David A, Lefef J, Murray RM.. Insight and neuropsychology in first-onset schizophrenia and other psychoses. *Schizophrenia Research,* 36(1-3): 145. 1999.

Young DA, Davila R, Scher H.. Unawareness of illness and neuropsychological performance in chronic schizophrenia. *Schizophrenia Research*, 10:117-124. 1993.

David A. van Os J. Jones P. Harvey I. Foerster A. Fahy T. Insight and psychotic illness. Cross Sectional and longitudinal associations. *British Journal of Psychiatry*. 167(5):621-8. 1995.

Fennig S. Everett E. Bromet EJ. Jandorf L. Fennig SR. Tanenberg-Karant M. Craig TJ. Insight in first-admission psychotic patients. *Schizophrenia Research*. 22(3):257-63. 1996.

Dickerson FB. Boronow JJ. Ringel N. Parente F. Lack of insight among outpatients with schizophrenia. *Psychiatric Services*. 48(2):195-9. 1997.

Poor insight is one of the strongest predictors of a poorer course of illness and medication noncompliance.

Many studies have found poor insight to be one of the strongest predictors of poor prognosis. Outcome variables studied include symptom exacerbations, "relapse," number and duration of hospitalizations, social and occupational dysfunction, overall quality of life and medication noncompliance (See reviews in: Amador et. al., 1991; 1993 for earlier literature).

Amador XF, Strauss DH, Yale SA, Flaum M, Endicott J, & Gorman JM. Assessment of Insight in Psychosis. *American Journal of Psychiatry,* 150:873-879. 1993.

See review in: Amador XF & Strauss DH. Poor insight in schizophrenia. *Psychiatric Quarterly*, 64:305-318. 1993.

Bartko G., Herczog I. & Zador G. Clinical symptomatology and drug compliance in schizophrenic patients. *Acta Psychiatrica Scandinavica,* 77:74-76. 1988.

McEvoy JP, Applebaum PS, Geller JL, Freter S. Why must some schizophrenic patients be involuntarily committed? The role of insight. *Comprehensive Psychiatry,* 30:13-17. 1989.

Bartko G; Herczog I & Zador G. Clinical Symptomatology and Drug Compliance in Schizophrenic Patients. *Acta Psychiatrica Scandinavica,* 77:74-76, 1988.

Caracci G; Mukherjee S; Roth S & Decina P. Subjective Awareness of Abnormal Involuntary Movements in Chronic Schizophrenic Patients. *American Journal of Psychiatry,* 147:295-298. 1990.

Cuesta MJ & Peralta V. Lack of Insight in Schizophrenia. *Schizophrenia Bulletin,* 20:359-366. 1994.

Ghaemi NS & Pope HG, Jr. Lack of Insight in Psychotic and Affective Disorders : A Review of Empirical Studies. *Harvard Review of Psychiatry,* May/June: 22-33. 1994.

Greenfield D; Strauss JS; Bowers MB & Mandelkern M. Insight and Interpretation of Illness in Recovery from Psychosis. *Schizophrenia Bulletin,* 15:245-252. 1989.

Heinrichs DW; Cohen BP & Carpenter WT, Jr. Early Insight and the Management of Schizophrenic Decompensation. *Journal of Nervous and Mental Disease,* 173:133-138. 1985.

Lysaker PH; Bell MD; Milstein R; Bryson G & Beam Goulet J. Insight and Psychosocial Treatment Compliance in Schizophrenia. *Psychiatry,* Vol. 57. 1994.

McEvoy JP; Appelbaum PS; Geller JL & Freter S. Why Must Some Schizophrenic Patients be Involuntarily Committed ? The Role of Insight. *Comprehensive Psychiatry* 30:13-17. 1989.

McGlashan TH; Levy ST & Carpenter WT, Jr. Integration and Sealing Over: Clinically Distinct Recovery Styles from Schizophrenia. *Archives of General Psychiatry*, 32:1269-1272, 1975.

Michalakeas A; Skoutas C; Charalambous A; Peristeris A; Marinos V; Keramari E & Theologou A. Insight in Schizophrenia and Mood Disorders and its Relation to Psychopathology. *Acta Psychiatrica Scandinavica*, 90:46-49, 1994.

Swanson Cl, Jr.; Freudenreich O; McEvoy JP; Nelson L; Kamaraju L & Wilson WH. Insight in Schizophrenia and Mania. *The Journal of Nervous and Mental Disease*, 183:752-755, 1995.

Wciorka J. A Clinical Typology of Schizophrenic Patients Attitudes towards their Illness. *Psychopathology*, 21:259-266, 1988.

McEvoy JP, Apperson LJ, Applebaum PS, Ortlip P, Brecosky J, Hammill K. Insight in schizophrenia. Its relationship to acute psychopathology. *Journal of Nervous and Mental Disorders*, 177:43-47. 1989.

Heinrichs DW, Cohen BP, Carpenter WT.. Early insight and the management of schizophrenic decompensation. *Journal of Nervous and Mental Disease*, 173(3):133-138. 1985.

McGlashan TH & Carpenter WT Jr.. Does attitude toward psychosis relate to outcome? *American Journal of Psychiatry*, 138:797-801. 1981.

Amador XF, Flaum M, Andreasen NC, Strauss DH, Yale SA, Clark SC, & Gorman JM. Awareness of illness in schizophrenia and schizoaffective and mood disorders. *Archives of General Psychiatry*, 51:826-836. 1994.

Kampman O. Lehtinen K. Compliance in psychoses. *Acta Psychiatrica Scandinavica*. 100(3):167-75, 1999.

Level of insight is not always associated with the severity of other symptoms:

Smith TE. Hull JW. Santos L. The relationship between symptoms and insight in schizophrenia: a longitudinal perspective. *Schizophrenia Research*. 33(1-2):63-7, 1998.

Amador XF, Flaum M, Andreasen NC, Strauss DH, Yale SA, Clark SC, & Gorman JM.. Awareness of illness in schizophrenia and schizoaffective and mood disorders. *Archives of General Psychiatry,* 51:826-836. 1994.

See review in: Amador XF & Strauss DH. Poor insight in schizophrenia. *Psychiatric Quarterly*, 64:305-318. 1993.

See review in: Amador XF; Strauss DH; Yale SA & Gorman JM. Awareness of Illness in Schizophrenia. *Schizophrenia Bulletin*, 17:113-132, 1991.

McEvoy JP, Apperson LJ, Applebaum PS, Ortlip P, Brecosky J, Hammill K. Insight in schizophrenia. Its relationship to acute psychopathology. *Journal of Nervous and Mental Disorders*, 177:43-47. 1989.

Poor insight is more often related to brain dysfunction, than defensiveness:

Just prior to the publication of the DSM IV, the hypothesis that awareness deficits in schizophrenia (particularly unawareness of symptoms) stem from neurocognitive deficits rather than psychological defensiveness was gaining currency (Amador et al., 1991). Since that time, multiple studies using insight measures with demonstrated reliability and validity have been published confirming the hypothesis. Most, though not all, of these studies have found this relationship to exist independent of variations in I.Q.. Three published studies have <u>not</u> found the hypothesized relationship between level of insight and frontal lobe function. However, because these studies measured very different aspects of unawareness than the studies listed below, and one of the studies had low statistical power, they are not considered failures to replicate.

Other studies have found structural brain abnormalities to be associated with lower levels of insight into illness. Although no negative findings have been published, the finding that certain structural abnormalities are associated with aspects of poor insight is preliminary as it is based on only two studies (Takai et. al., 1992 and Flashman, 1999). No statement regarding structural abnormalities of the brain and insight has been added. Nevertheless, these findings are mentioned here, as they are consistent with the proposition that in most cases, poor insight is related to brain dysfunction rather than psychological defense.

Also consistent with this proposition are studies reporting that approximately one half of schizophrenia patients with tardive dyskinesia (TD) lack awareness of the specific signs and symptoms of TD, and are unaware of having a movement disorder more generally. This form of unawareness is not accounted for by lower I.Q. or clarity of consciousness.

Mohamed S. Fleming S. Penn DL. Spaulding W. Insight in schizophrenia: its relationship to measures of executive functions. *Journal of Nervous & Mental Disease.* 187(9):525-31, 1999.

Morgan KD, Vearnals S, Hutchinson G, Orr KGD, Greenwood K, Sharpley R, Mallet R, Morris R, David A, Leff J, Murray RM. Insight, ethnicity, and neuropsychology in first-onset psychosis. *Schizophrenia Research*, 36(1-3): 144. 1999.

Morgan KD, Orr KGD, Hutchinson G, Vearnals S, Greenwood K, Sharpley M, Mallet R, Morris R, David A, Lefef J, Murray RM. Insight and neuropsychology in first-onset schizophrenia and other psychoses. *Schizophrenia Research*, 36(1-3): 145. 1999.

Young DA, Zakzanis KK, Baily C, Davila R, Griese J, Sartory G & Thom A. Further Parameters of Insight and Neuropsychological Deficit in Schizophrenia and Other Chronic Mental Disease. *Journal of Nervous and Mental Disease,* 186: 44-50. 1998.

Lysaker PH. Bell MD. Bryson G. Kaplan E. Neurocognitive function and insight in schizophrenia: support for an association with impairments in executive function but not with impairments in global function. *Acta Psychiatrica Scandinavica.* 97(4):297-301, 1998.

Voruganti LN. Heslegrave RJ. Awad AG. Neurocognitive correlates of positive and negative syndromes in schizophrenia. *Canadian Journal of Psychiatry.* 42(10):1066-71, 1997.

McEvoy JP. Hartman M. Gottlieb D. Godwin S. Apperson LJ. Wilson W. Common sense, insight, and neuropsychological test performance in schizophrenia patients. *Schizophrenia Bulletin.* 22(4):635-41, 1996.

Kasapis C, Amador XF, Yale SA, Strauss DH, Gorman JM, Poor insight in schizophrenia: Neuropsychological and defensive aspects. *Schizophrenia Research*, 15:123. 1995.

Lysaker P, Bell M, Millstein R, Bryson G, Beam-Goulet J. Insight and psychosocial treatment compliance in schizophrenia. *Psychiatry,* 57 (4): 307-315. 1994.

Young DA, Davila R, Scher H. Unawareness of illness and neuropsychological performance in chronic schizophrenia. *Schizophrenia Research*, 10:117-124. 1993.

Correlations between abnormal brain structure and insight:

Takai A, Uematsu M, Ueki H, Sone K and Kaiya Hisanobu. Insight and its Related Factors in Chronic Schizophrenic Patients: A preliminary Study. *European Journal of Psychiatry*, 6:159-170, 1992.

Flashman LA, McAllister TW, Saykin AJ, Johnson SC, Rick JH, Green RL, Neuroanatomical Correlates of Unawareness of Illness in Schizophrenia. From the Neuropsychology & Brain Imaging Laboratories, Dept. of Psychiatry, Dartmouth Medical School, Lebanon, NH & New Hampshire Hospital, Concord, NH 03301. Presented at the *Biennial Meeting of the International Congress on Schizophrenia Research*, Santa Fe, New Mexico, April 20, 1999.

Poor Insight into Tardive Dyskinesia:

Caracci G; Mukherjee S; Roth S & Decina P. Subjective Awareness of Abnormal Involuntary Movements in Chronic Schizophrenic Patients. *American Journal of Psychiatry*, 147:295-298, 1990.

Arango C. Adami H. Sherr JD. Thaker GK. Carpenter WT Jr.   Relationship of awareness of dyskinesia in schizophrenia to insight into mental illness. *American Journal of Psychiatry.* 156(7):1097-9, 1999.

Alexopoulos GS. Lack of complaints in schizophrenics with tardive dyskinesia. *Journal of Nervous & Mental Disease.* 167(2):125-7, 1979 Feb.

Sandyk R. Kay SR. Awerbuch GI. Subjective awareness of abnormal involuntary movements in schizophrenia., *International Journal of Neuroscience.* 69(1-4):1-20, 1993.

Selected Summaries of Articles Cited

Amador XF, Flaum M, Andreasen NC, Strauss DH, Yale SA, Clark CC, & Gorman JM. Awareness of Illness in Schizophrenia and Schizoaffective and Mood Disorders. Archives of General Psychiatry, (51): 826-836. 1994.

The study reported in this paper involved over 400 patients from around the country and showed, unequivocally, that poor insight into illness is common in psychotic disorders while being rare in other psychiatric disorders. Large proportions of patients with schizophrenia, schizoaffective disorder, psychotic mania and psychotic depression were generally unaware of having an illness. This study is the first to also evaluate whether patients with these disorders were aware of the signs and symptoms of illness that they personally suffered from. Again, a very large proportion of patients in each of these four groups had no insight into the signs of the illness that they had despite the fact that they had been hospitalized in order to receive treatment for the very same symptoms that they were unaware of. The results of this study make it clear that many patients with these disorders lack the ability to recognize that they are ill and in need of medical care.

**Sandyk R. Kay SR. Awerbuch GI. Subjective aware-
ness of abnormal involuntary movements in schizophrenia., International Journal of Neuroscience. 69(1-4):1-
20. 1993.**

A majority of schizophrenia patients with tardive
dyskinesia, a neurological disorder produced by chronic
neuroleptic therapy, lack awareness of their involuntary
movements. This by contrast to patients with Parkinsonism
who usually are aware of their abnormal movements. In
this paper the authors report on a series of studies aimed at
providing further insight into the issue of awareness of
involuntary movements in schizophrenia patients with tardive dyskinesia. In addition, they investigated whether
edentulosness, which may be a risk factor for orofacial
dyskinesias in the elderly, is also a risk factor for neuroleptic-induced orofacial dyskinesias. They found that: one's
awareness of involuntary movements is related to some but
not all muscle groups, tardive dyskinesia may be associated
with a significant distress, lack of awareness may be a feature of frontal lobe dysfunction in schizophrenia, patients
who lack awareness of their involuntary movements have a
higher prevalence of pineal calcification, and edentulosness, which is related to deficits in the orofacial sensorimo-
tor system, increases the risk for neuroleptic-induced orofacial dyskinesias.

**Amador XF; Strauss DH; Yale SA; Gorman JM &
Endicott J. The Assessment of Insight in Psychosis. *The
American Journal of Psychiatry*, 150:873-879. 1993.**

This paper reports on a reliability and validity study of
a new scale for assessing various aspects of insight into illness. Five years after the publication of this article, the
Scale to assess Unawareness of Mental Disorder (SUMD)
has become the most widely used instrument for assessing
insight into illness in psychiatric research. It has since been
translated into fifteen languages by psychiatric researchers
world-wide reflecting a new consensus that the scientific
study of insight is possible. The study reported in this paper

found that patients with schizophrenia and schizoaffective disorder had pervasive problems with awareness of being ill and that particular aspects of poor insight were strongly correlated with non-adherence to treatment while other aspects of unawareness were not. Similarly, a poorer course of illness and the number of previous hospitalizations were also correlated with various aspects of poor insight. On the other hand, level of education and level of positive and negative symptoms of the illness were unrelated to insight suggesting that deficits in illness awareness are not a consequence of educational background or simply the byproduct of other symptoms of psychosis. The authors conclude that insight has multiple dimensions than can, and should, be measured reliably. And that deficits in insight are a separate and independent sign of the illness that affects adherence with treatment and the overall course of schizophrenia.

Young DA; Zakzanis, KK; Baily C;. Davila R; Griese J; Sartory G & Thom A. Further Parameters of Insight and Neuropsychological Deficit in Schizophrenia and Other Chronic Mental Disease. *Journal of Nervous and Mental Disease*, **186, 44-50. 1998**.

This more recent study of 108 patients with schizophrenia, found, once again, strong correlations between various tests of frontal lobe function and level of insight. Using the Scale to assess Unawareness of Mental Disorder (SUMD), Young and his colleagues found significant correlations between percent of perseverative errors on the Wisconsin Card Sort Test and overall awareness of illness and attributions for specific symptoms as measured by the SUMD. In this study bipolar patients were also examined using the same methodology, however no significant associations between the insight measure and tests of frontal lobe performance were found. These results replicate previous findings that support the idea that poor insight into illness and resulting treatment refusal stem from a mental defect rather than informed choice in patients with schizophrenia.

ective functions.

Lysaker P. Bell M. Insight and cognitive impairment in schizophrenia. Performance on repeated administrations of the Wisconsin Card Sorting Test. *Journal of Nervous & Mental Disease.* **182(11):656-60. 1994.**

Research has suggested that poor insight in patients with schizophrenia is associated with poorer treatment compliance and outcome. Little is known about the etiology of poor insight. Poor insight has been attributed to a willful preference for illness, a psychological defense, and cognitive impairments. To test the hypothesis that poor insight is related to enduring cognitive deficits, the performance of 29 patients with schizophrenia and impaired insight and 63 patients with schizophrenia and unimpaired insight was compared on repeated administrations of the Wisconsin Card Sorting Test. Results indicate that subjects with impaired insight demonstrate consistently poorer performance over a period of 1 year than subjects with unimpaired insight. When the effects of I.Q. were partialled out, subjects with impaired insight made significantly more perseverative errors and achieved fewer categories correct, a pattern of performance deficits identified with neuro-psychological dysfunction in schizophrenia. These results support the hypothesis that cognitive impairment may underlie poor insight in schizophrenia.

Mohamed S. Fleming S. Penn DL. Spaulding W. Insight in schizophrenia: its relationship to measures of executive functions. *Journal of Nervous & Mental Disease.* **187(9):525-31. 1999.**

Lack of awareness of specific symptoms among persons with schizophrenia has not been adequately studied in the context of neuropsychological function. The purpose of this study was to investigate whether poor insight as measured by the Scale to Assess Unawareness of Mental Disorder is empirically related to performance measures having a known association with executive functions (frontal lobe function) in a group of individuals with chronic schizophrenia. The results showed that unawareness and misattribution of negative symptoms are significantly associated with deficits in some aspects of executive functioning even after a test of general intelligence had been partialed from the analyses. The researchers conclude that unawareness of negative symptoms is associated with executive functioning in individuals with chronic schizophrenia. Unawareness of other symptoms (i.e., positive symptoms) may reflect dysfunction in other types of neuropsychological processes, or it may reflect motivation to deceive oneself or others.

Kasapis C, Amador XF, Yale SA, Strauss D, Gorman JM. "Poor Insight in Schizophrenia: Neuropsychological and Defensive Aspects, *Schizophrenia Research*, **20:123.1996.**

This paper reports on a replication of the Young et. al., study which implicated frontal lobe dysfunction in the etiology of poor insight in patients with schizophrenia. The study also investigated the extent to which defensiveness might play a role in such unawareness. The authors (XFA) had previously hypothesized that frontal lobe pathology may account for the severe forms of unawareness frequently seen in certain psychotic disorders. This study tested this hypothesis using the same neuropsychological tests and insight scale used by Young and his colleagues. Defensiveness was measured using the Balanced Inventory of Desirable Responding (BIDR). The results indicated that defensiveness was modestly correlated with only a handful of the different measures of poor insight. On the other hand, the neuropsychological test results were nearly identical to that of Young and colleagues, indicating that poor performance on tests of frontal function predicted poor insight independent of other cognitive functions tested including I.Q. This independent replication adds further evidence in support of the idea that poor insight into illness and resulting treatment refusal stem from a mental defect rather than defensiveness or informed choice.

Smith TE. Hull JW. Santos L.   The relationship between symptoms and insight in schizophrenia: a longitudinal perspective. *Schizophrenia Research.* **33(1-2):63-7. 1998.**

It has been suggested that deficits in symptom awareness and attribution in schizophrenia are relatively independent of core symptoms of the disorder. Many studies report conflicting findings, however, which may be explained by differences in study design and target population. In this study, 33 individuals with schizophrenia or schizoaffective disorder were assessed longitudinally using standard symptom and insight measures, with analyses focusing on associations with psychotic, depression and anxiety symptoms. Both cross-sectional and longitudinal analyses showed significant but only moderate associations between insight and symptoms of depression and disorganization, with no consistent relationships with positive and negative symptoms. Higher levels of depression were associated with improved awareness and attribution, whereas higher levels of disorganized symptoms were associated with deficits in awareness and attribution. The results are compared with the previous literature, and it is suggested that insight deficits in schizophrenia may vary depending on factors such as course and phase of illness.

Arango C. Adami H. Sherr JD. Thaker GK. Carpenter WT Jr.   Relationship of awareness of dyskinesia in schizophrenia to insight into mental illness. *American Journal of Psychiatry.* **156(7):1097-9. 1999.**

The purpose of this study was to determine whether lack of awareness of motor dysfunction and lack of insight into mental dysfunction are related and to evaluate the longitudinal stability of lack of awareness of abnormal movements in schizophrenia. Forty-three patients with schizophrenia and tardive dyskinesia participated in the study. The Scale of Unawareness of Mental Disorder was used to assess insight. All patients still meeting inclusion criteria after 2 years (N = 16) were reevaluated at follow-up.

Twenty (46.5%) of the 43 patients had at least moderate unawareness of their tardive dyskinesia. Awareness of tardive dyskinesia was only modestly related to two of the five dimensions of insight into mental disorder assessed. Patients with the deficit syndrome showed significantly less awareness of their tardive dyskinesia than patients without the deficit syndrome. Lack of awareness of tardive dyskinesia was stable over time. The authors conclude that lack of awareness of tardive dyskinesia is a common feature in schizophrenia and is stable over time. Since patients are often unaware of dyskinesia, direct clinical examination is required to identify early tardive dyskinesia.

Lysaker PH; Bell MD; Milstein R; Bryson G & Beam Goulet J. Insight and Psychosocial Treatment Compliance in Schizophrenia. *Psychiatry*, Vol. 57. 1994.
Unlike most studies of insight in the chronic mentally ill, this study evaluated patients when stabilized and enrolled in an outpatient work rehabilitation program. Patients with schizophrenia and schizoaffective disorder with poor insight had very poor adherence to the psychosocial treatment they had agreed to participate in despite a stated desire to work. Poorer insight was also correlated with lower scores on a test of frontal lobe function and with poorer performance on tests of other cognitive functions. The authors conclude that individuals with schizophrenia and poor insight have more problems remaining in a course of treatment regardless of whether it is pharmacologic or a psychosocial treatment they had expressed a desire to participate in. These data, like that of Young et. al., and Kasapis and colleagues, suggest that it is a mental defect that leads to lack of adherence with both pharmacologic and psychosocial treatments.

McEvoy JP, Freter S, Everett G, Geller JL, Appelbaum
PS, Apperson LJ & Roth L.). Insight and the Clinical
Outcome of Schizophrenic Patients. *Journal of Nervous
and Mental Disease*, 177(1): 48-51. 1989.

Patients with schizophrenia were followed from 2 to
3 years after discharge from the hospital. Although symptoms of psychosis improved in nearly all of the patients
over the course of the initial hospitalization, improvement
in insight was seen only in those patients who had voluntarily agreed to being hospitalized. Patients who had been
involuntarily committed to the hospital did not show a similar improvement in level of insight into the illness.
Furthermore, the low levels of insight persisted throughout
the follow up period only in those patients who had been
involuntarily admitted to the hospital. Not surprisingly,
these same patients were more likely to be involuntarily
committed over the course of follow up. The authors conclude that an inability to see oneself as ill seems to be a
persistent trait in some patients with schizophrenia and one
that leads to involuntary commitment.

Young DA; Davila R & Scher H. Unawareness of
Illness and Neuropsychological Performance in Chronic
Schizophrenia. *Schizophrenia Research*, 10:117-124.
1993.

This study reports on data that implicates frontal lobe
dysfunction in the etiology of poor insight in patients with
chronic schizophrenia. Previous authors had hypothesized
that frontal lobe pathology may account for the severe forms
of unawareness frequently seen in certain psychotic disorders (see recommended review article: Amador et al., 1991).
Young and his colleagues tested this hypothesis using neuropsychological tests and the Scale to assess Unawareness of
Mental Disorder (SUMD). The results indicated that poor
performance on tests of frontal function predicted poor
insight independent of other cognitive functions tested
including IQ. These results lend important support to the

idea that poor insight into illness stems from cognitive dysfunction rather than informed choice or defensive denial.

**Amador XF; Strauss DH; Yale SA & Gorman JM.
Awareness of Illness in Schizophrenia.** *Schizophrenia
Bulletin*, **17:113-132, 1991.**

This paper reviews the extant literature on insight into
illness (up to 1991) in schizophrenia. The authors argue for
a reassessment of the problem and consensus on terminology and measurement with the stated goal of stimulating scientific research. Furthermore, they argue that poor insight
in patients with schizophrenia may be due to brain dysfunction. They point out numerous similarities between
poor insight in patients with schizophrenia and anosognosia
(a neurological syndrome characterized by unawareness of
illness) in neurological patients. Multiple studies link poor
insight to noncompliance with treatment, poorer course of
illness, increased hospitalizations, involuntary commitment,
poorer social and occupational function, but not with positive symptoms of the disorder. They conclude by offering
guidelines for terminology and research.

**McEvoy JP. Hartman M. Gottlieb D. Godwin S.
Apperson LJ. Wilson W. Common sense, insight, and
neuropsychological test performance in schizophrenia
patients.** *Schizophrenia Bulletin*. **22(4):635-41, 1996.**

The authors report on an exploratory study examining
the interrelationships among common sense, insight into
psychosis, and performance on a battery of neuropsychological tests in 32 patients with schizophrenia evaluated at
the time of discharge from involuntary hospitalization at a
State psychiatric hospital. Common sense, as measured by
the Social Knowledge questionnaire, was associated with
better performance across tests measuring parietal lobe
functioning and vocabulary. In addition, patients with more
common sense were more likely to say that they were ill
and needed treatment. A global measure of insight, the

Insight and Treatment Attitudes Questionnaire (ITAQ), was related to performance on a test of left parietal lobe function. However, the responses to the ITAQ item that may best reflect current awareness of mental illness in patients at the time of discharge ("After you are discharged, is it possible you may have mental problems again?") were related to performance on tests of the functioning of the prefrontal lobes and the right and left parietal lobes. These results add to the growing evidence that some of the deficits in awareness of illness among patients with schizophrenia are related to the neuropsychological dysfunction commonly seen in patients with this disorder.

Amador XF & David A, Eds. *Insight and Psychosis.* **Edited volume, Oxford University Press, 1997.**
    In this book the neurological basis of deficits in illness awareness is the focus of several chapters that extensively cite empirical studies published in peer reviewed journals. In addition, data indicating that lower levels of insight are associated with poorer illness course, increased exacerbations of illness, greater number and longer duration of hospitalizations and non adherence to treatment are reviewed. The role poor insight might play in violent behaviors is also discussed at length.

Improving Insight with "Video Confrontation"
    A recent study at McLean Hospital by Davidoff and colleagues demonstrated that patients exposed to a videotape of his or her own psychotic behavior gained significant improvements in insight into their illness. Although the idea to use videotape to increase insight into illness has been in the research literature for thirty years there has been almost no work in this area. In *Videotape Techniques in Psychiatric Training and Treatment*, Berger (1970) discusses the findings of Cornelison and Arsenian (1960); "Self-image confrontations were influential in bringing about rapid changes in psychotic patients." They also hypothesized that "Self-confrontation may bring a psychot-

ic individual into better contact with his realistic self."

Berger further observed, " Seeing oneself and reflec-
tively re-experiencing meaningful interactions frequently
allows a person to acknowledge something about himself
which he had not previously been ready to accept from
either the therapist or others in the group. Confrontations
enable patients to identify their own self-defeating patterns...to join the therapist in a pro-therapeutic position. It
is as if the process tends to demand the giving up of blind
spots and denial systems. Further, where change is
achieved, patients are often best able to see it in the play-
back session, when they can be more objective."

In 1998, after nearly 25 years, a study by Dr. Stephanie
Davidoff and a team of researchers at Mclean Hospital re-
introduced the concept of "video self-observation" (VSO) as
a therapeutic tool in psychiatry. Their research successfully
demonstrated the positive effect of video self-observation on
insight in subjects recovering from psychosis. They hypothesized that, "Exposing partially remitted patients to videotapes
of themselves, made while they were acutely psychotic,
might increase their insight into the nature of their illness."

Acutely psychotic inpatients were assigned randomly
to a control or experimental group and interviewed on
videotape shortly after admission. Subjects were interviewed using the Insight and Treatment Attitudes
Questionnaire (ITAQ) and the Brief Psychiatric Rating
Scale (BPRS) to measure insight and psychopathology.

After receiving standard hospital care, and when
judged to be significantly improved, subjects in the experimental group were shown videotapes of their initial interview, and subjects in the control group saw a placebo
videotape. All subjects were then re-evaluated using the
ITAQ and BPRS.

Comparisons of the initial and final ITAQ and BPRS
scores revealed a significantly greater improvement in
insight in the experimental group that was not achieved by
the control group. The researchers concluded that, "Video
self-observation...may be a cost-effective therapeutic tool

for developing personal insight into psychotic illness."
They suggested that, "...future studies are needed to evaluate whether the effects...are reproducible, persist over time,
and result in an improvement in treatment compliance."

Prior to the publication of Davidoff, *et al*, Robert
Gallaher, a relative of someone with serious mental illness
and head of the Rainbow Research Group, independently
developed and tested a remarkably similar hypothesis. That
effort was motivated by an experience summarized in the
following anecdotal narrative:

> A man, I will call Greg, diagnosed with
> schizoaffective disorder agreed to be videotaped
> in his home during a severe and prolonged psy-
> chotic episode. He exhibited poor awareness of
> his illness and consistently refused treatment
> over a period of several years involving multiple
> relapses.
>
> A short time later, he was involuntarily com-
> mitted to a psychiatric hospital. Greg received
> standard hospital treatment including the admin-
> istration of risperidone and lithium, and quickly
> recompensated. After 17 days, he was released to
> his family's care under a 90 day court order for
> out-patient treatment. Toward the end of the 90
> day period, he stated he was now "fine" and
> would discontinue
> treatment when the court order expired.
>
> Following this declaration, Greg agreed to
> view the videotape made prior to his hospitaliza-
> tion. Shortly after this video self-observation
> experience, he volunteered that he was aware,
> for the first time in his life, that he suffered from
> a mental illness and that he now understood the
> need for his medication.
>
> Greg made the following comments when
> asked how he felt about this experience and
> whether he thought it might benefit others:

"Video shows you acting in a way that you
normally wouldn't do, and saying things you
wouldn't normally say...It would show people
after they are normal how they were before...it
gives them insight into what they were
like...You can't get that insight any other way
except by seeing how you were...It is capturing
that moment in time when you weren't doing
good...It hits you consciously and unconsciously
by seeing yourself in that state...When you're
better, you would never know how you were
before if you couldn't see for yourself...If you
see yourself on TV — It's the one chance you
get to look at yourself."

As a result of this experience, an application was
made to the NAMI Research Institute to study the use of
video self-observation as a tool to improve insight and
treatment adherence. That study was funded in 1999 and is
currently running at Stanford Medical Center.

If successful, the results of the current study will provide additional evidence of the positive effect of video self-
observation on insight and awareness of illness in patients
with psychotic disorders. The researchers further anticipate
uncovering a direct correlation between video self-observation and improved treatment adherence. A significantly
larger, multi-site study that includes follow-up measure-
ments of insight and treatment adherence over a much
longer term is planned to confidently answer the questions
raised by these initial studies. My research group will be
participating in this study and I have high hopes that this
technique can be added to our arsenal of interventions
aimed at increasing insight.

Berger MM: *Videotape techniques in psychiatric training
and treatment*. New York, Brunner/Mazel, Inc. 1970,
Chapter 2

Davidoff SA, Forester BP, Ghaemi N, Bodkin JA: Effect of video self-observation on development of insight in psychotic disorders. *J Nerv Ment Dis* 1998; 186(11):697-700

Cornelison F, Arsenian J: A study of the responses of psychotic patients to photographic self-image experience. *Psychiatric Quarterly* 1960; 34:1-8

About

Xavier Amador

and

Anna-Lisa Johanson

XAVIER AMADOR has a brother, Henry, who has schizophrenia. Dr. Amador is the Director of Psychology at the New York State Psychiatric Institute and a Professor of Psychology in the Department of Psychiatry at Columbia University College of Physicians & Surgeons. He is a world renown expert on the problem of poor insight into illness in individuals with schizophrenia and bipolar disorder. He has published over 60 scientific articles and his work in this area has been translated into 16 languages by scientists worldwide.

Dr. Amador has appeared on numerous television programs as an expert in this area and on mental illness more generally (NBC's Today Show, Good Morning America, CBS This Morning, NBC Nightly News, CBS 60 Minutes, CNN, NBC Dateline, Fox News Channel, Court TV, A&E Network, Discovery Channel and PBS among others). He has been interviewed by the New York Times, U.S.A. Today, Los Angelos Times, Reader's Digest, The New Yorker, and many other publications. He has consulted to the National Institute of Mental Health, Veteran's Administration, the U.S. Attorney General's Office and other government agencies involved in mental health research.

He is a practicing psychotherapist in New York City and has published three previous books: *When Someone You Love is Depressed: How to help your loved one without losing yourself* (Simon & Schuster); *Being Single in a Couples' World* (Simon & Schuster); and *Insight and Psychosis* (Oxford University Press).

ANNA-LISA JOHANSON is the daughter of Margaret Mary Ray, the woman most people know as "David Letterman's stalker." Her mother, diagnosed with schizophrenia and schizoaffective disorder, took her own life in the Fall of 1998.

Ms. Johanson is finishing her law degree at Georgetown University Law School and is pursuing a career in mental health advocacy. She works part time for the Treatment Advocacy Center in Arlington, Virginia, where she assists in developing legal resources for consumers and families of the seriously mentally ill. She has written for Glamour magazine and has appeared on NBC's Dateline to talk about the problems serious mental illness creates for families. She lives with her husband in Washington D.C..

Index